The New Rules
of Customer Engagement

6 Trends Reinventing the Way We Sell

The New Rules of Customer Engagement

6 Trends Reinventing the Way We Sell

© 2014

By Daniel L. Newman

Cover art design by Katie Stockham

ISBN: 978-1-63173-435-9

First Printing: 2014

BroadSuite
T. 817-480-3038
http://broadsuite.com

http://millennialceo.com/book

Advance Praise for
The New Rules of Customer Engagement

As a marketer who is always looking at what is happening today, but also what is coming next, I genuinely appreciate the conversation Daniel is having with business leaders about the role of information, social business and customer advocacy in the B2B space. Dan's ideas on how B2B is shifting to a true Peer to Peer conversation is one I strongly believe in. And as a marketer I aspire to have many of these conversations with our customers and employees everyday.
—*Michael Brenner, Blogger, Speaker and VP Marketing & Content Strategy, SAP*

In a world where the entire customer experience from start to finish is changing faster than most companies can adapt, business leaders need practical insights that can be quickly understood and implemented. Daniel provides both the insight and the example for companies to stay ahead of the curve.
—*Skip Prichard, President and CEO, OCLC*

As the Director of Community for one of the worlds leading online media outlets, I am immersed everyday in the changes and trends in how people communicate. Daniel's book provides wonderful clarity on how businesses can better engage customers and build trust both on and offline even in the age of short attention spans and too much disposable information.
—*Tim McDonald, Director of Community – Huffington Post*

The pace of change in the business world, fueled by new business models driven by social media, has been incredibly fast and relentless. We're living in a very different world of work, but not all employees have internalized what that means for their careers. The big change is that customers are empowered. They won't respond to sales tactics that were effective even five years ago. Daniel Newman's new book, The New Rules of Customer Engagement, gets at the heart of how people need to change to stay relevant in their careers. Newman puts his pointers in the context of today's reality: businesses need to meet the customer's need rather than sell services or wares based on marketing's 'Wow' factor.

—Meghan M. Biro, Founder and CEO – Talent Culture & Forbes Top HR Influencer

As an entrepreneur that helped pioneer technologies that help business people turn who they know into how they grow, I found Dan's insights on the shifting sale to be spot on and his focus on customer experience critically important. In the future, business success will be determined by how we build and maintain authentic and relevant connections with the right customers, at the right time on the most effective channel to build, nurture and maintain mutually beneficial business relationships.

—Jon Ferrara, CEO Nimble and CRM Pioneer (Founder of Goldmine)

Call off the dogs. The debate as to how much the consumer-driven world we are in has changed, is over. The consumer is in charge and no one knows that better than Daniel Newman whose latest book is absolutely a must-read for businesses and brands of any size who have any hope of being in business in the years to come.

—Steve Olenski, Forbes and Business Insider Contributor. Top 100 Social Media Influencer

To rise above the noise in today's cluttered digital world, a message must have something that was once a luxury (but it now a necessity: it must be interesting <u>and</u> actionable. In his book, Dan provides critical insights and a fascinating perspective on the trends that are changing how customers do business. Looking for a roadmap to navigate through today's endlessly changing trends? Get this book. It's <u>how</u> today's entrepreneurs and executives stay true to themselves while gaining control of these economic and cultural shifts.

—*David Brier, Chief Gravity Defyer, DBD International, Fast Company expert blogger and award winning branding consultant*

Table of Contents

Why This Book, Why Now?

For those that don't know me well, my business passion has always lied around technology and that is why I chose to build my career in the audiovisual (AV) and collaboration technology space.

When I first decided to write this book, it was about providing practical insights and actionable business strategies to the industry in which I spent the first 12 years of my career. As the project progressed, it became increasingly apparent that this book and the change it represents isn't just for those in the audiovisual industry, but rather for any business large or small that seeks to get closer to its customers.

The New Rules of Customer Engagement will explore the most important trends, six in fact, that are reinventing the way businesses of all types should be selling to their customers. It dives into how the buyer's journey is changing and what your business can do to stay ahead of curve.

Partnering with *Commercial Integrator*, a leader in business insights to the audiovisual and technology systems integration community, we pulled from some of the best business minds in the industry to build a book that not only serves our industry, but can quickly and easily be related to just about any business or industry.

When this project started it was about helping businesses transform and that is exactly what I hope this book does.

Entrepreneurs, business leaders and sales professionals alike, if your role is creating better customer experiences, this book is for you. See you on the other side.

Forward by Tom LeBlanc

Does the guy that I'm about to describe ring familiar to you?
He works on your sales team.

He's a long-time veteran that helped build the company up to where it is now.

He's a sharp dresser, but his clothes seem to be from another era.

He describes himself as a "phone guy" and eschews email communication when possible.

He's funny; during tense points in meetings he's the guy who breaks the silence with a witty remark.

He appears to dismiss the Internet as something that's abstract, counter-productive and some sort of hipster fad.

He knows everybody's name within the company and is extremely well-liked.

If I worked with you, this guy would be one of my favorite co-workers. So I take no pleasure in writing that I think he's holding back your company.

It's overwhelmingly evident that the way integration firms must approach sales has changed. The old adage that sales associates ought to "always be closing" has evolved to "always be demonstrating return on investment." (I don't think ABDROI will catch on, however.)

The integration industry, which is extremely progressive in terms of system design, often lags behind when it comes to elevating the sales process. Those two factors aren't mutually exclusive. Sales associates within integration firms are, understandably, enamored with their company's solutions. They lead with the "wow," which was probably the right approach a few years ago.

Now their clients can easily find the "wow" with a quick Google search. They can see the "sizzle" by watching Youtube videos. What they want, primarily, from their integration firm is to understand how those sensational solutions can translate to a positive impact on their firm's bottom line.

Will it increase productivity? How?
Will it save on overhead? How much?
Will it drive additional business? When and from where?

What it boils down to is that sales professionals at integration firms need to focus on conveying how important they are to their clients — and it goes without saying that their companies needs to back up those claims with actual value. The problem, however, is that most integrators aren't very good at conveying that value, articulating clear ROI in the form of metrics.

Security integrators are perhaps better than their IT- and AV-centric competitors. Warrendale, Pa.-based Vector Security, for instance, understands that "as integrators, we have to change our business focus from hardware and software to how the customers can benefit post-installation," says Art Miller, VP of marketing. "How will this help them solve their business issues, reduce risk, increase their bottom line? We need to be providing them with business intelligence that is beyond the contacts at the door or the cameras in the hallway."

For AV-centric integrators, finding the formula for providing clients with valuable on-going information and conveying it isn't as obvious — but it's still critical. "It's a little harder on the AV side, but it's absolutely important for companies to maximize their profitability. That's where they've got to go," says NSCA executive director Chuck Wilson, adding that logical areas in which AV integrators can provide and communicate money-saving metrics for clients relate to building automation, energy management and life safety. "It's hard to show ROI sometimes, but [integrators] are getting better at it."

Normal, Ill.-based Zdi doesn't see any choice but to become good at articulating ROI, according to CEO Aaron McArdle. "As opposed to getting somebody to spend $200K on a board-room because it's cool, we have to be able to provide [ROI] that affects the company's bottom line. If you can add to a conference room the ability to show how often the room is used and how many people are typically using it, the company can adjust accordingly." That may seem esoteric, but for a client that has 300 conference rooms it can lead to significant savings.

"I think of AV as kind of in a juvenile stage," says integration firm member group USAV president K.C Schwartz. "It's time we grew up into young adulthood as an industry and start thinking about our role in demonstrating business value, not just running around talking about projectors."

This is an area in which there is a clear need for traditional integrators to evolve beyond selling boxes, says InfoComm executive director David Labuskes. "I get it, the boxes are important. I value the boxes. I value manufacturers. They're providing technology and appliances that allow us to accomplish and provide the types of solutions our clients need. But that's only one part of the solution. If you focus your efforts on that part, you're forgoing the opportunity to be part of the strategy of the client," he says.

Those strategies, Labuskes continues, have almost nothing to do with products. "Years ago we used to say [to clients], 'You need this display because it has all these great features.' Now we're saying these great features will result in this type of performance. What you need to be saying now is, 'This performance will impact the quality of your meetings, and the quality of your meetings will result in better decisions, which will make you a more competitive organization, or will help you heal people better, or will help you educate people better." Regardless of the mission, you have to apply what you're providing to a client to how they're achieving their mission."

For integration firms, meanwhile, their mission is critical: Evolving their sales processes to the point where it's as sophisticated as the solutions they provide. That's why I welcomed Commercial Integrator columnist Daniel L. Newman's idea to write a book on the "New Rules of Customer Engagement."

Dan is taking on a subject that is critical for integration firms — *Commercial Integrator's* primary audience. Sitting back and not revisiting sales strategies is no longer a viable option for integrators.

In his book, Dan digs into six trends that he says have altered the way sales professionals need to engage their clients. Like me, you might not agree with every single one of his points, but Newman — who draws on experience that includes a stint as CEO of Chicago-based United Visual – forces us to rethink sales conventions and push forward.

Even if you disagree, even if it makes you angry, you won't regret reading.

Tom LeBlanc, editor-in-chief
Commercial Integrator

Chapter 1:
New World, New Rules

Imagine a world where you never had to break a sweat to sell anything.

Everyday the ideal number of clients with perfectly aligned needs to what you have to offer would just walk through the door and shout out, "I'll take it!"

Could business get any better? Any easier?

If you're a business person — particularly one that sells goods and services to other businesses, B2B, accustomed to arduous sales cycles — that seems like a pipe dream.

But what if I told you that "I'll take it" phenomenon is already happening? Well, sort of – it isn't quite so simple and the customers aren't really just arriving sight unseen ready to buy whatever it is you are selling. But it is happening.

Think of the steps you take upon realizing that it's time to purchase a new car.

What's the first thing that you do?

Do you hop in your old car and drive over to the local dealership?

Perhaps you pick up the newspaper and see what special savings are being offered?

You *could* do either of those things, but if you were like the vast majority of people today you would do neither.

You'd most likely take your iPad off the charger, head over to your sofa, put your feet up on the ottoman and start surfing.

You would find your way through the car review sites, perhaps check the manufacturer sites to see if they have any special offers and incentives and then finally you might pop onto Facebook to ask for your friends opinions on the cars that you have put on your short list.

Once you have your research done you have now determined the following:

- Which car you want
- What features you would like it to have
- How much your exact car should cost, MSRP and Invoice
- Edmunds' target price to pay
- Your trade in value via Kelley Blue Book
- Your credit standing courtesy of Experian
- Your approximate interest rate and payment amount from bankrate.com
- Potential car loan options by applying on a competitive lending site and received multiple offers

You're ready to walk into the dealership with a printout in hand of the vehicle you want, the value of your trade, the price, interest rate and a pre-approved loan and say, "Bring my new car around."

Essentially you walked in to the dealership and bought what they had to offer for the price that they want to sell it for and you are going home happy. Like magic, only it isn't.

What you just experienced is the new way of doing business: New rules, new engagement.

Only now, these rules are impacting everything, not only how we as consumers buy things personally, but how businesses consume as well.

B2B, B2C, P2P, it doesn't matter; we are all consumers

looking to buy in a new economy, an informed economy. It is scary, exciting and one heck of an opportunity for businesses to prosper.

LOOKING AT THE NUMBERS BEHIND THE CHANGE

Guess how many information sources, on average, that a buyer engages with prior to making a purchase.

What do you think? Two? Three? Five?

What if I told you the number is 11.4?

According to Google, buyers on average engage with more than 11 pieces of content prior to making a purchase decision and, according to a study by Forrester Research, that number has doubled year over year in each of 2012 and 2013.

Furthermore, we have entered a day where consumers don't trust advertising.

Although we are now exposed to over 5,000 advertisements per day, the consumer really doesn't trust advertisements.

Instead the new consumer seeks to make purchase decisions through word of mouth and brand engagement via social platforms and native advertising (content marketing).

In fact, 90 percent of consumers trust a recommendation from their network and 81 percent of those go online to get those recommendations. On the other hand there isn't a single type of advertising that consumers trust at a rate of greater than 50 percent with many forms of advertising being trusted at rates in the 20-30 percent range.

Bottom line, not only is the way we are consuming changing, but our reference points are evolving rapidly and trust is proving to be a precious commodity.

WHAT IS THE RETURN ON TRUST?

If I were a business and I knew by gaining the support of a key group of influencers that we could achieve greater success in word-of-mouth marketing would I make gaining their support a priority?

You are darn right I would!

That 90 percent of buyers trust a network referral is critical. It leaves us as businesses to ask, who represents the network and how do I gain the support of those influencers to evangelize my business.

> *What is crazy is that even though 98 percent of business owners say that word of mouth is their lead driver of new business, only 3 percent of businesses have a strategy to capitalize on this.*

This means that most businesses simply aren't pursuing the support of the brand influencer.

Why?

Why go through the heavy lifting of building trust one by one when you can build a virtual army of ambassadors to support your brand?

Is it too hard?

Perhaps you don't know where to start?

What if I told you that this group of loyal supporters is right in front of you? They are those already buying from you and those that have worked with you in the past whom had good experiences. While they may not be able to bring you all the business you can dream of, they can each bring one or a few who bring another few and suddenly ... You have arrived.

In the new economy this is all possible. Building a business where clients are banging on the door because they want to work with you may seem difficult or impossible, but it isn't.

We are in a new economy with new rules that favor not those who have done it longer or spent more money, but those that know what their customers need and how to deliver it to their satisfaction.

Are you ready for what is next? Welcome to *The New Rules of Customer Engagement*. Understanding the six trends that have redefined successful sales processes can be the difference between being left behind or staying a step ahead of your competitors — the difference between thriving partnerships with customers and, well, former customers.

DO YOUR CUSTOMERS VALUE WHAT YOU DO?

Visualizing Real Value vs. Perceived Value

For anyone out there that has children (or has ever been a child, for that matter), think about a time when someone bought you a really nice gift that you didn't want. Maybe it was a piece of jewelry that you would never wear or a cashmere sweater that isn't your style.

It's difficult to muster a "thanks."

This is a perceived **value**. Regardless of the price of the item, because the recipient doesn't care for it, the *value* is extremely low. That is because <u>value</u> directly correlates with the recipient's want or need for the item(s).

Why You Must Understand What Is Valuable to Your Customers

Applying the example above to the work that we do, allow me to ask a question:

Have you ever dealt with a client or customer that doesn't value what you do for them?

Another question:

Have you ever felt that no matter how hard you try, the work you do will never be good enough and feel like you constantly have to reinforce the value that you bring?

Pretty frustrating, right?

Of course it is. You work hard to satisfy your client and in return you get no appreciation. Perhaps only the financial gain offsets the disturbing nature of the relationship. But we deal with it because it is part of business, right?

Here is the thing ...

I know that businesses need to take on work that isn't ideal at times to keep the lights on. However, there is a question you must ask yourself each day: What value do my customers and, for that matter, each customer see in the product or service that is provided?

The answer should be at the forefront of everything you say and do for your customer. And if for some reason you don't have a good answer for this question, perhaps their disdain or ungrateful nature is more warranted than you think.

Learning What Customers See as Valuable

So what do you think is the easiest way to find out what is valuable about your services to your clients?

While you can probably discern this to some degree by the services most rendered, that really only indicates what your organization is best at selling.

I suggest the best way to learn what your customers see as valuable would be to ask them.

It amazes me how often I have dealt with clients or been a client and never been asked for feedback. And whether that feedback is in some type of survey or, more ideally for a smaller business via a face-to-face discussion, it is paramount that we ask our clients and customers what they see as value that we deliver.

The Most Important Thing to Understand About Value

If you were going to take one thing away from this book, I would hope it would be this...

Real value that drives long-term business relationships is built when the client believes that the value they are getting for products and services exceeds the amount of financial compensation that they are paying for those services.

Believe it or not, it is really that simple. Even if you are offering what you feel is a great deal for your service, if it isn't what the client needs, it isn't worth what you are asking.

It all goes back to the really nice sweater that Grandma bought you. She could have told you it was a thousand dollar sweater, and the only thing that could have made you smile was knowing you could return it or exchange it for something that you want.

In the simplest form, that is value.

Moving forward, ask yourself this with every customer you serve. Are we creating the type of value that is going to keep customers happy and working with us?

Introduction: Death of a Sales Professional

To imply that sales is becoming irrelevant is, to say the least, bold, and an explanation is needed.

In the world of business, **sales** have long been the lifeblood of the organization. From the first customers to where a business is today, the success of *sales* attributes much to the achievement of the organization.

This is precisely why <u>sales</u> professionals are usually the highest paid employees within the organization, often making two to three times more than the operations, finance and marketing managers which are the ones behind the scenes helping them to get the job done.

Having said that, sales also tend to carry the most risk. Often a substantial portion of their income is tied to their performance (directly and indirectly) as well as their ability to keep customers when projects go awry. However, the ability to keep the customers isn't so much a sales role as it is a customer service role, which is why the end of the sales pro, at least as we know it, may be upon us.

Networking = New Sales; Google = New Yellow Pages

When you want to buy a house, a car or a new flat-panel television, who do you call? Oh wait, you don't call anyone. You research on Google.

You call your friends and ask them what they have.

That's the "New Sales" and it is how we consume things today. And it is how the buyers of just about every product on the planet consume today.

It's a growing trend, given that buyers today engage with twice as much online content as just one year ago (according to Forrester). This means a company's ability to market online is the new sales, and the role of the traditional sales person has really just become customer service.

Is that a bad thing? It is for some people who have been the "trusted advisor." But like everything, times are changing and there is just no way a sales rep can keep up with the changes as well as Google and the trusted communities of the buyers.

Sales Will Never Fully Go Away, But Change Is Imminent

Some people probably won't like that I'm saying this, and I'm okay with that. Gone are the days of the high margins on commodities and consumables, we have entered the day of the "New World Sales," a place where margin and profit is determined by the value you bring and customer experience you create.

This means sales needs to focus more on managing customer relationships, delivering unparalleled service and being highly available when they are needed.

These aren't necessarily new items, rather they were items that would be neglected when talking about new technology and live demos took precedence. But the consumer as we knew it has been lost, absorbed into a world where Google answers their questions and social/ trusted networks fill the voids.

The good news, however, is that with every great change comes great opportunity. Now that the customer is armed with as much information as we have, we can turn our attention back to nurturing the relationships through great customer experience.

So *sales* aren't going away. It is just changing. Leaving businesses to ask themselves, how will your organization embrace the shift?

SOURCES:

Digital Buzz Blog, "Social Consumer"
http://www.digitalbuzzblog.com/infographic-the-social-consumer/

Prophet.com, "Transformation"
http://www.prophet.com/sites/transformation/infographic.html

Nielsen
http://1.bp.blogspot.com/-12dl_z0AG8k/T4sG-qrxP0I/AAAAAAAABOU/Ri1F-hqdQzlY/s1600/nielsen%2Bad%2Btrust%2B4.2012.pptx.jpeg

Forrester Research
http://blogs.forrester.com/lori_wizdo/12-10-04-buyer_behavior_helps_b2b_marketers_guide_the_buyers_journey

6 TRENDS DRIVING THE NEW RULES OF CUSTOMER ENGAGEMENT

If you lead a business, any business, B2B or B2C, things are changing.

Not only in the way have we meet our customers' needs, but the entire process. Shift is underway.

From the first contact until eternity, it is the responsibility of our organizations — large and small — to create memorable customer experiences. Not some of the time, but all of the time.

In a world cluttered with mediocrity, standing out is the only way to get ahead and stay there. In fact, I content that average customer experience is worse than bad.

So how do we better engage our customers?

For most companies this isn't going to happen by chance. It takes acute recognition of the changes happening around us.

Beyond recognition, it will also take action by leadership — a conscious shift from decision-makers to embrace the change and implement new ways of doing things in just about every part of their businesses.

Perhaps you think you know what these changes are, or maybe you are wondering if the shifts we are going to explore are the same as certain shifts that you see in your business.

So what is changing?

I call them "The New Rules of Customer Engagement." These rules are constructed by the impact of six business trends happening around all of our businesses that may or may not be obvious day in and day out.

One by one, we will explore six trends that are forever changing the customer engagement process, then we will lead thought provoking conversations that can be applied to your business, and leave you with resources for implementing the new rules to your business.

These six trends shape how companies need to do business from this day forward:

Trend 1: *How Informed Consumers Are Changing Everything*

Trend 2: *Why Your Response Time Must Be Faster: The Impact of immediacy on Customer Experience.*

Trend 3: *Getting Creative – Your Business Value Lies In Your Creativity*

Trend 4: *The Role of The Human Network; Your Human Network*

Trend 5: *Don't Sell Me. Show Me! Selling more by driving outcomes and Advocacy Within your Client Organizations*

Trend 6: *Customer Experience Trumps Everything Else You Do: Why Mediocre is the New Bad and Extraordinary must be the Ordinary.*

If your business is ready to take on the changing landscape impacted by these six trends, stay with us as we explore how to create better business outcomes every day by focusing first on what todays customers are seeking from their suppliers.

Ready to go?

We look forward to connecting to better customer experiences with you.

Chapter 2:
Trend: Informed Consumers Are Changing Everything

DISSECTING THE NEW CONSUMER: MORE INFORMED, MORE EXPOSED

Are you participating in the first 70 percent of the sale?
Did you know that a client needs to be exposed to a message three to five times before they will trust it? That's according to a 2012 survey performed by Edelman.

How often do your sales executives get three to five shots at making a sale?

In today's rapidly growing technology driven marketplace, consumers are doing more of their own research and that is creating a major shift for sales people. Most notably, it is changing the point in the sales cycle where sales professionals even enter the conversation. The effects of this are critical.

How Information Creates Late Sales Entry
In the hay day of sales, the client would have their "Trusted Advisor" that would come in and guide the organization's technology adoptions.

The expectations of this trusted advisor were that they knew what technology was out there, that they had access to demonstration of product, that they would offer competitive/fair pricing and, of course, that they were able to install the technology once it was procured.

With this set of priorities it made the role of the sales person invaluable to the organizations that they served. They were needed to enter the sales process very early so they could help with needs analysis, introduction and vetting of products and ultimately the sale and implementation.

For technology sales this has done a 180 in the past few years. **Tech buyers are now engaging with on average more than 10 pieces of online content prior to even starting their process of sourcing a supplier.** This means that they are about 70 percent into their buying decision prior to including a sales person.

Does this trend impact your business?

Think about it. Are your customers more or less often dictating the technologies they want implemented when you are brought in to deliver a proposal?

If the answer is "more," you are likely experiencing the effects of the more informed customer that is doing more of their own research through online and social networking. This shift unfortunately means that your role as trusted advisor might be less substantial than it once was.

That doesn't mean you should give up; it means you should change the way you approach this new breed of consumer.

Working With Highly Informed Consumers

Do you fancy yourself as a highly informed consumer? When buying your cars, televisions or smart device, do you walk into the store and say, "Help me?" or do you walk into the store and say, "Here is what I need?"

I'll bet most of you aren't the former. Like your clients, you scour the web and ask friends what their experience has been with "XYZ" product. Do you think your clients are different? Probably not.

To work with highly informed consumers you need to do one of two things.

1. Come prepared to take their knowledge and turn it into something more useful (Problem Solving)

2. Be the source of the knowledge.

Ideally you will do both of these things, but sometimes it is hard to control where the consumption of information comes from. However, if you want to have more control early in the sales process it is a great idea for your organization to be doing the education early and often.

Do you want your clients to buy the newest unified communication platform? Then make education readily available through online content, live events, webinars and of course the face to face sales meeting.

(Note: When you do get those meetings make sure you are coming with some valuable ideas. Lunch doesn't cut it anymore!)

In cases where you can't get ahead of the curve, the key is making sure the value that you bring solves clients' problems beyond just knowing what technology they need.

If the client thinks they want a video solution from Cisco, help them figure out how to deploy it as widely as possible so they can get video on the desktop, in the huddle rooms and on mobile devices rather than just in the boardrooms and conference spaces.

Sales professionals who can take their clients knowledge and make it more valuable will long have their place, but beware the informed consumer is changing everything and it is the first of six trends that are transforming the tech sale for the foreseeable future.

HOW TO REGAIN YOUR TRUSTED ADVISOR ROLE

If the Internet has really taken over the role of first responder, how in the world do B2Bs regain their roles as trusted advisors? After all, it was that coveted role that long made your company the first person they would call when a need arose.

People didn't go to Google or ask their friends on Facebook. They called *you* and said, "We have a need. Can you help us?"

Here is the thing ... Google hasn't actually taken the role of trusted advisor. Google merely indexes pages of companies that provide relevant information based on what is being searched.

So while it may be harder to be the first person that a company calls, it isn't impossible.

In order to regain the role of trusted advisor you need to do two things better than you did them before:

1. Anticipate your customer's needs:
2. Provide information proactively

Anticipating Customer's Needs: When it comes to being a trusted advisor in the new economy it means you have foresight that your clients may not. In a lot of cases your clients are busy doing very specific things for their company.

Say your company sells software based telepresence to the enterprise. For one particular client you know the IT director has responsibility for implementing a version of the service or solution that you sell (potentially yours or a competitor's solution). For all you know your solution is No. 8 on its list of priorities, meaning they are doing very little proactive research on the topic. However, it is still on the list!

Within that example, here is where your opportunity lies. Knowing that your item, while not the highest priority, is indeed a priority you can reach out and say "Hey Mr. IT Director, I know telepresence is among your list of priorities for 2014. Our company is a leading provider and I would love to provide you with an overview of several of the leading offerings in this technology space."

While not all customers are going to jump on this, many busy IT executives with 10-plus priorities would love to have someone doing their homework for them. Of course, it comes with certain risk to give away your expertise, but you and I both know that the information you will ultimately share is going to aid in your marketing cause.

If you focus on taking the opportunity to provide quality information you will not only be the person that provided that intelligence, but you will quickly take steps toward being the trusted advisor — which in today's world starts with anticipating your clients' needs.

Proactively Distributing Information: On the heels of anticipation is the actual delivery of useful materials to the prospect/client.

These materials may be blogs, case studies, videos or product specifications.

The actual content will often vary depending on the stage of the purchase in which the client is.

What we know for sure is that building trust with the client is easier if you augment your ongoing selling efforts with content.

The numbers tell the story here:

- 70 percent of consumers prefer to get to know a company through reading their articles rather than advertisements. *[Source: Forrester Research]*
- 60 percent of consumers feel more positive about a brand after reading custom content on their site. *[Source: Forrester Research]*

What this says, in short, is by being the source of useful information you are breaking down trust barriers and providing the client a way to become informed without having to aggressively sell to them.

Ideally, the content is generated by your organization to show thought leadership and technical aptitude; however, that doesn't always have to be the case. I often share compelling infographics with clients that show the impact of customer retention, digital marketing or cloud adoption.

Many times I share it unprovoked and I will usually include a short anecdotal reason for sharing:

- "Based on our conversation the other day about cloud ..."
- "You had mentioned an interest in learning more about SEO, so ..."

Surprisingly (or maybe not), these more informal little shares tend to bring tremendous returns both in response and conversion. **It is when you balance understanding your customers' needs and providing them with the information they need to reach a purchasing decision that we return to our role as trusted advisor.**

To share without purpose is as ineffective as not sharing at all.

Remember, the ultimate goal is to provide information that

makes your client more knowledgeable about the ultimate product or service they will be purchasing while simultaneously earning their trust so they buy it from you.

FORGET SEARCH ENGINE, DRIVE CONTENT

Another hotly debated topic for SMBs is Search Engine Optimization (SEO). Landing on the first page of Google for certain keyword searches is the Holy Grail for most businesses. However, it isn't realistic or likely for most businesses that SEO will be a viable solution, at least not in the traditional sense.

Since this book covers a lot of ground on the importance of a changing breed of consumer who does more of his or her research online, it made sense to provide a little bit of detail on what SEO is and how it should be looked at by the vast majority of B2Bs. Let's call this an SEO crash course before we move on to several other topics where SEO may pop into your head as a viable solution for selling to the informed consumer.

SEO in the Past

Take everything you have ever heard about SEO and chuck it! Well maybe you don't have to go that far. Chuck that, too. But here is the thing.

If you are looking to build a site that Google loves and has you showing up on the first page every time, maybe it is time to realize the rules have changed a little bit.

In the past, search was impacted by one thing more than anything else: Link building.

It was Link Building efforts that kept SEO and PPC marketers focused because it was the quantity and more importantly the *quality* of links that was going to drive page rank up and therefore position in a Google search.

After Link Building, SEO was heavily focused on formatting. SEO experts would turn their attention to using the keywords in the right header tags (H2, H3) and then splattering the keywords throughout the content and using italics, Bold and underline to further improve search rank.

Link building is still very important, but some other factors have become immensely important and B2B Marketers need to take notice.

SEO Today: Quality Content, Socially Authoritative

One of the first topics my clients ask about is SEO. How do we drive SEO to be found on Google?

While the traditional SEO items I mention above are important, I usually take clients down a different route. This route covers two areas:

- Their content strategy and marketing efforts as well as their social media, curating and sharing strategy
- SEO and the role of content

I ask clients if they have a blog. If so, I ask if they keep it up to date with quality content driven to answer their prospective clients' most important questions about the solutions they offer.

If they say no, I know we are starting at zero.

Even the most optimized B2B site if just a static products and services website will have a hard time growing and sustaining traffic.

Wondering just how important content is? Check out this Searchmetrics visual aid showing the content factors driving search (on page 25).

In short, to improve in almost all of these areas you need more high quality content.

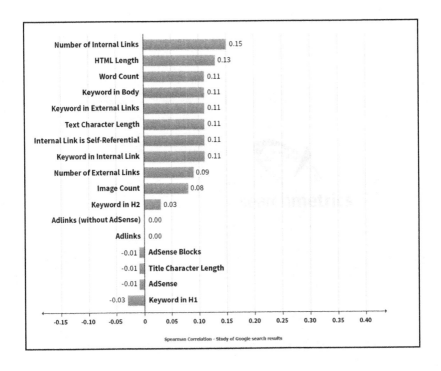

Spearman Correlation - Study of Google search results

SEO and the Role of Social Media Signals

I then ask clients ...

"How does your organization use social media?"

"Are you consistently sharing the content you are (or aren't) creating across the platforms?"

"Do you curate and share other useful content to build trust and relationships with potential clients interested in similar subject matter?"

"Is your brand engaged and having conversations with readers in your target audience?"

The purpose of these questions is to determine if their brand is social and if it has an engaged community of any sort that shares content.

It's important, because here is a little secret of SEO that most

B2Bs don't realize: Social Sharing is a huge driver of SEO!
Need proof? Check out this second study from Searchmetrics.

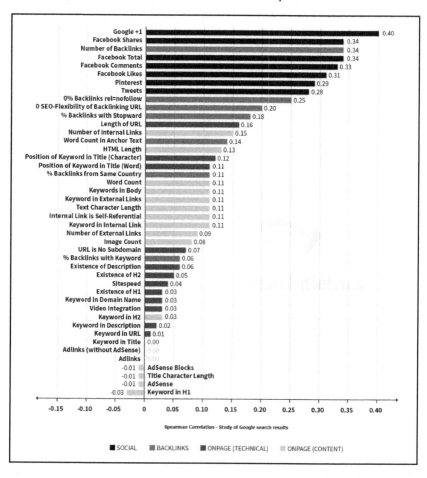

Notice anything here? Seven of the top eight factors driving SEO are social sharing related and not traditional SEO drivers whatsoever!

Want SEO? Drive Content, Get Social

For companies asking themselves the old, "How do we improve SEO?" question, the answer is simpler than you may think. The challenge for businesses is that unlike in the past where the building process was more about following steps, grabbing backlinks and properly formatting content, the rules have changed.

If you want better SEO, you need to create more content and drive it through social channels. It really is (or isn't) that simple.

SOURCES:

Content Marketing Institute
http://contentmarketinginstitute.com/2012/02/best-content-marketing-infographics

ENTERING AN ERA OF LESS B.S.
By Chuck Wilson

We now live in a transparent world where no B.S. is allowed or tolerated. The need for honesty and truth in every sales pitch is now mandatory. Likewise, facts can be checked almost instantly in side-by-side product comparisons. We now have to know the facts and not the assumptions.

Pricing is a constant concern. Sales associates like their managers have to know the exact spot where their "minimum mark" on each and every transaction is. They need to be complimented, not criticized, for walking away from an order below that mark.

Selling value, not price is the goal. And it is hard, very hard to do.

The most frustrating words a sales associate can here is, "We can buy that for far less on the Internet." At NSCA, our members constantly ask what would be a good response to that. Let's try this:

Sales person: "And who will install and provide the warranty?

Client: Our IT staff can install those display and cameras when they aren't busy with programming or networking problems.

Sales person: OK. Sounds like you are all set and will be saving some money doing it yourself. Call me when you need something else. Oh, one more thing, I didn't realize your IT folks were trained on this type of system and that you had workers' comp insurance that covered programmers being up on ladders installing displays.

Client: Wait a minute, what was that last part?

The point of that story is we need to keep educating our sales associates on all the little things that provide a value, such as the SOC codes that insurance companies use to manage workers' comp insurance rates/claims and so on. Once we lay all that out, often times the "do it internally" option doesn't seem so attractive. And that is just one example out of dozens we can offer.

If your sales associates quotes a product that can be bought off the Internet without first checking the Internet themselves, what should happen next? That's right, you bring them in for sales training 101. If it happens the second time you set them free.

Customers will always want to itemize and price out hardware. Good sales people will want to bundle and package. So what happens when your sales associate says, "our policy is not to break out the pricing? We offer only an installed price with labor and warranty included." The client fires back, "We only buy on price and need everything itemized."

What should be running through the sales person mind is this: "I represent a value-added systems integration company who offers advanced technology solutions to allow your business to excel in what you do and for you to focus on what you do best."

What is really running through their mind is: "I wonder how much trouble I would be in to take 10 points off this deal?"

The reaction to this should be driven from the company culture and from the top down. Rarely have I ever seen a company who is successful at being both a value-added integration firm and a low cost box sales company. In fact, I don't know of any who are still in business. The overhead, cost structure and selling expenses just doesn't allow it anymore.

I'd say the biggest adaptation for the sales associate to this transparent world we live in is them requiring additional sales training and education on overcoming objections to the low price versus best value methods of selling. Even really good sales people could become much better by adapting to the new type of client they deal with and using updated methods suited for selling solutions rather than product.

Chuck Wilson is executive director of National Systems Contractors Association.

"Buyers are more knowledgeable now. With that, you really have to step up your game. If you're just focused on price, you're going at this the wrong way."
—Dale Bottcher, Western Region VP of Sales, AVI-SPL

"It's not just about purchasing people going online and doing spot checks on large ticket items. It's also that he consumer market is driving the commercial market, which also leads to the margin eroding. You need to emphasize your differentiators."
—Bill Chamberlin, VP of Sales, Verrex Corporation

"The biggest impact [of customers doing more research before engaging an integrator] has mainly been unfair comparisons of product based purely on price and not feature sets. The overall effect has been the commoditization of technology which is not best serving the client."
—Bruce Kaufmann, President & CEO, Human Circuit

The biggest impact from customers doing more research before engaging an integrator is "no longer answering questions about the products, but what can this solution do for my organization? That takes a very different approach to making a sales call, and you need to be well prepared. Websites hold all of the product information, along with pricing, which is easily attainable by the end user, so simply talking about specs is no longer an option."
—Michael Boettcher, CEO, Advanced AV

"It's critical to understand the client's intent for receiving quote from us. The questions we ask are, 'Is this a sole-source bid or are you planning to put this out to multiple bidders?' If the question comes back sole-source we take our clients at face value and with details. If the answer comes back [multiple bidders] will give them a quote lacking many of the precise details that would allow the customer to go out and just do their own shop online or give the information to our competitors. In the case of sole-source quotes we'll often let the client know they were going to charge them a design fee and that will roll that design fee back off the project costs and into the bottom line once they decide to give us a PO for the project."
—**Rod Andrewson, *Manager of Engineering and Project Management Services, CCS Presentation Systems***

"We all grown up in AV and that's where we've cut our teeth but we're now squarely a video communications provider. The folks we deal with are no longer the facilities managers. I don't know when the last time was that we dealt with one of those guys. Those roles don't really exist anymore. Our contact are more in the IT division."
—*Dale Bottcher, **Western Region VP of Sales, AVI-SPL***

Chapter 3:
Your Response Time Must Be Faster

THE IMPACT OF IMMEDIACY ON CUSTOMER EXPERIENCE

Social Media and Connected Consumers Shift Service Wait Times to Near 0

How often does a 2 p.m. or 3 p.m. service call come from a client and you think to yourself, "That can wait until tomorrow"?

You're not alone in having that reaction. However, what if I told you that 67 percent of customers expect same-day response to their service requests online (via social media)?

That expectation puts two wheels in motion that directly impact your business. First, customers are expecting faster response times; second, social signals are rapidly moving into not just other industries but yours as well.

This evolving trend that started primarily with B2C where customers would use social media as a channel to get quick response times to service needs — and to publically complain — is quickly migrating toward the B2B space.

In the same study that revealed the 2/3 metric mentioned, it was found that 42 percent of consumers expect a response not just in the same day, but within one hour. Meanwhile, a staggering 32 percent expect it in 30 minutes.

Even more problematic, these expectations are being set around the clock. The consumer doesn't care what time of day it is.

Applying the Numbers to B2B Companies

I'm sure some B2B organizations are thinking that those numbers don't apply to us. It does, but I need to go on a little tangent to explain how.

Remember when the iPhone first came out and everyone wanted to use it for work, but IT departments said no? The company had its standard issue Blackberry or similar device and that was what IT was approving for use.

We all collectively thought to ourselves that the iPhone is so much more user friendly with great applications and more web-friendly. At the time, however, it didn't matter. If you wanted an iPhone, it was on you to buy it and support it.

Then suddenly a monumental shift occurred. We're seeing less Blackberry use by companies, and iPhones are the corporate issue phone of choice (in many organizations).

What happened?

User demand is what happened. Consumerization is what happened.

People from CEO's to the rank and file demanded a change, and IT departments had to figure out how to make it work.

Now back to customer experience and how this relates. The shift from the Blackberry to the iPhone was all about better customer experience. It was driven from the consumer side and the expectation was set by trending technology that people use.

Guess what ...

There are over a billion people on Facebook and 50 percent of them log in every day. Additionally there are over 300 million on Twitter, LinkedIn and other large social media platforms.

Given that 29 percent of the users are logged in at work, I would say that the B2B client is well represented in this mass of users and therefore the B2B customer is the social media consumer.

How Does This Affect Customer Experience Expectations?
Not to oversimplify, but the connection is going to become more and more obvious.

What people expect in their personal lives is immediacy in response to their complaints. However, what they will grow to expect in their professional lives is much the same.

The B2B consumer is also the B2C consumer. This has always been the case, but it hasn't been until recent years that personal user experience began to lead enterprise user experience and that this has become such an impact for businesses.

The expectations, in essence, have been flipped upside down. Customers' B2B expectations are being driven by their B2C experiences.

For your business, it isn't unrealistic that your customers are expecting a level of immediacy that you have never seen before.

What you may be finding is that they aren't telling you about it yet, or they are looking for a provider that can deliver the experience they expect at which point they will switch.

It is up to today's B2B organizations to make themselves available to deliver service at the next level.

Whether that means 24x7x365 call centers, social media monitoring and management or some other method of continuous accessibility, one thing is for sure: The rules are changing.

Businesses looking to thrive in the connected economy must respond faster as we quickly approach "zero" as the only acceptable wait time for response to service needs.

THE CHANGING LANDSCAPE OF B2B OFFERING SERVICE AGREEMENTS

Should B2Bs be rethinking service contracts and delivery?

Somewhere in history a very wise businessperson came up with the concept of sign this service contract and for the next year we will deliver you the services entailed.

Caveat: Even if I don't deliver to the expectation we set, for the next year we will continue to send you a bill every month until the contract is up.

Second Caveat: Around 10 months into the contract we will show up and ask you to renew your contract. If you don't, our service levels will further diminish because we will need to turn our attention to clients who are still under contract.

Oh, the irony.

Source: *successwithcrm.com*

So you sign up for a contract to receive a guaranteed level of service for a period of time; however, even if you don't get service that meets your expectation, you are stuck in the agreement.

Whoever came up with this idea was definitely smart, but

were they customer experience focused?

Shifting from Commitment-to-Pay to Commitment-to-Perform

I know that some service providers will argue that the service contract they deliver includes service level agreements or at least specific performance spelled out.
Before you assume those commitments are worth the paper they are written on, ask two questions:

1. Who set the service agreements?
2. Who wrote the contracts?

The contracts are almost always pro-provider and they are often written in a way where the provider's expectations are far lower than the goal of service should be.

The real question becomes: Are we in a marketplace where contracts are required?

In large industries like mobile telecom and cloud services there is already a tangible shift moving contracts from long-term to month-to-month. Sure, there may be a small price to pay for clients to get out of their contracts and dealing with change itself is often an immovable force, but why do you think this shift is happening?

Performance-Based Agreements Will Rule Future

When I started my business as a content and digital marketing service provider, I decided not to require long-term contracts. Everything is based on 30-day agreements. Considering it takes months sometimes to see ideal results I recognized the need for short-term agreements.

My No. 1 priority has to be client satisfaction. This needs

to be the No. 1 priority for any business. Rather than focusing on how you can lock a customer in and hold them captive, reinvest that energy into ways to make them happy each and every day.

This is the future of service delivery — customer experience.

With so many organizations catching onto the idea of earning the opportunity to serve and then providing the service, the old-school service "contract" may have a short shelf life ahead.

The good news is satisfied clients almost always stay. So if your business truly is about continuously creating great customer experiences, you really don't have much to worry about.

And sure, I get the concerns with moving away from service contracts; with a shift like this a certain level of discomfort will be created.

Remember, if you deliver in the end and the customer has a need for the service you provide, you should be in great shape. Most of the time when they leave it isn't because they don't need your service; it is because your service let the customer down.

Nonetheless, whether the idea of the "no-term" contract sounds brilliant or asinine, it is the way of the future in a "show-me" economy.

Learning Resource: A Drip Theory for Improving Customer Experience and Retention

If customer experience is the No. 1 driver of retention, what are the little things that a business can do to create those lasting positive impressions?

We often think big when it comes to making a splash. However, sometimes when it comes to client retention it is the small things that really count.

For instance, many companies get fixated on automation. They look at each step on the sales and fulfillment process and try to drive automated activities to drive better results.

Does this resonate?

The problem with many processes is that the intention isn't to create better customer experiences but to increase profitability. When you squeeze the "human" out of the process you may be commoditizing rather than improving. At the very least, remember that automating isn't a replacement for high-touch. In most scenarios, process automation should be designed to free up time for humans to do more human things, like making sure their clients are happy.

Differentiate Delivering Great Customer Experiences

Remember the 80 and 8 rule (that 80 percent of companies think they are highly differentiated but only 8 percent of clients think their vendors are highly differentiated)? Well, no matter how well you think you are differentiating, you probably aren't. When it comes to service, though, there is a real case to be made for doing things that make customers happy.

Since keeping a customer is about six times cheaper than finding a new one let's make sure we don't let them walk out. To that point, creating real customer experience is more about a drip than it is about a storm.

If customer experience is being done under duress, the effort is often futile. How many instances can you recall when you ran to put out a fire and you think you have saved the day only to have the customer walk out the next day, week or month?

That is because it never should have gotten to that point in the first place.

There are always items that are out of your control, but more often than not when the house is on fire you either had the matches or the gasoline.

That is why deploying a drip theory is critical to creating better customer experiences. This "drip" should consist of two very important things: Responsiveness and being proactive.

Responsiveness: Never make a disappointed customer wait longer than necessary. Just reaching out to let them know exactly when they can expect to hear from you, can reduce a blow up. Just make sure that whenever you tell the client you are going to call that you absolutely do so.

Augment this by making sure your clients have real vehicles to reach you. Don't send them to a generic customer service inbox that you know only gets checked once a day.

When I was CEO of Chicago-based integration firm United Visual, I would give every customer my direct email, phone and cell number. If there was a problem I wanted them to know they could call me.

I learned two things from doing this:

1. Customers will rarely go around the process unless they have to;
2. Being this available won new customers and saved some rocky relationships.

While I never liked getting the calls and emails from really unhappy customers, I sure did like having the last chance to save a relationship.

One last note on responsiveness, whether your company likes social media or not, do not ignore social Channels as an opportunity to provide better customer experience for your clients.

With more than a billion daily users of social media customers are on Facebook, LinkedIn and Twitter. It is easy to set up these channels and it is also easy to listen to these channels.

More customers are using social to engage with brands *and* to voice issues when they arise. It is important that customers know your business is social and that you are paying attention to what they are saying there.

Given the shifting demographic of young millennial managers moving into influential positions, this trend will continue to impact consumer behavior. In fact, 49 percent of the workforce by 2020 will be millennials. With 80 percent of them being active in social, this isn't a fad. Social is pervasive and part of doing business.

Like all other communications channels, don't make the mistake of setting these up and ignoring them. It makes a business not only appear out of touch but it is also a great way to have a customer think they reached out only to be ignored.

Being Proactive: The biggest problem I see with customer experience delivery is that there is this immediate perception that customer service is something that happens only after a sale is complete.

This isn't true.

Customer experience has a lifecycle that starts from the very first time a potential customer engages with your business. This can be via a marketing campaign, a direct sales call or social media. It doesn't matter, but from that instant the clock is ticking.

This basically means there is a certain expectation of customer satisfaction from everyone in your CRM system and while the current paying customers always emerge at the top of the heap, that doesn't mean the others aren't listening and paying attention.

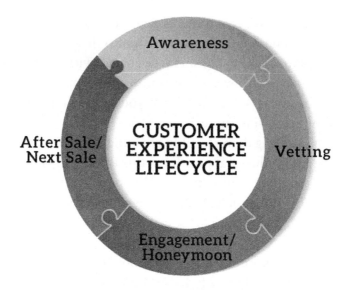

A "drip" approach is a perfect way to accommodate the real customer experience lifecycle and it can be managed by keeping tabs on the client proactively throughout the entire customer experience.

Awareness Phase: This is the part of the customer experience lifecycle where they are getting to know your company. This is a great time to touch them with useful content on related services, share valuable industry knowledge and invite them to events your organization may be attending. Sounds like sales, but this is also customer experience.

Vetting Phase: During the vetting phase a potential prospect has reached out and wants to get to better know your brand. Ideally, by this point, the drip has built some underlying trust and drawn the customer closer to your brand.

During this phase the responsiveness factor becomes super-important; however, this is just the beginning. We all know about the company that was hot on everything when they were trying to win the business only to disappear once they have the contract in hand.

Engagement/Honeymoon Phase: This point in the experience lifecycle is when the customer has agreed to do business with you on some level. This is when the talk ends and the delivery becomes paramount. During this phase a company needs to stay very responsive and be on the constant lookout for feedback. Waiting isn't an approach to find out if there is an issue. During the honeymoon period you are setting the bar for the rest of the relationship. Make it high-quality and sustainable. This is also a great place to focus on proactive expectation setting so miracles don't become an everyday expectation from the customer.

After Sale/Next Sale Phase: Once the first project done together is complete and the customer is happy, the cycle doesn't end. It actually returns to the beginning where that relationship is managed and the information drip begins to seed the workings of the next project together. In addition this is the continued service phase where making sure the client is continuously happy with the past work is equally as important as their desire to work on the next thing. Whatever your business does, don't be the company that only shows up on the day where there is an opportunity to sell. Customer experience is ongoing and those that treat it that way will emerge in the new economy.

TACKLING TRANSPARENCY:
TIME FOR BUSINESSES TO COME CLEAN

Repeat after me ...

"Our customers are smart. They may not know everything about everything, but they know a little bit about a lot of things."

Companies continuously try to treat consumers like they are stupid. On a recent day, as I write this, about 20 percent of sites on the Internet were down when leading hosting companies like Host Gator, Bluehost and others simultaneously (by chance?) went down. If only you could have seen the outcry on Twitter of companies trying to figure out what was going on with their website.

One of my sites is hosted on Bluehost, so this outage affected me. For hours all the folks at Bluehost would say is, "Sorry, about the outage. We are working hard to fix it." To their credit, they were responding to the flood of complaints at breakneck speed. However, they weren't saying anything useful, which bothered me.

Imagine ordering a pizza at the restaurant and it comes out cold; you tell the wait staff and they thank you for letting them know, but don't bring you a hot pizza!

Expediency in responding is not only a nice to have; it's a requirement in today's business. But there has to be some substance. You can't just feed everyone cold pizza and expect them to like it.

If I told you that 95 percent of consumers take action on negative customer experiences, would you believe me? It's true.

Of course, not all choose to leave, (note: 82 percent will leave a supplier at some point based on a bad experience), but what they do choose to do can certainly have an adverse effect on your business.

Let's take a look at how customers deal with their dissatisfaction:

- 85 percent want to warn others about doing business with your company

- 66 percent seek to discourage others from doing business with your company

- 55 percent look to vent by sharing their experience

- 24 percent seek for the company to resolve the issue

What this basically says is that an unhappy customer will almost always affect your business negatively in some way. Worse yet is that less than 1 in 4 of your customers are going to actively try to work with you to resolve the problem. The rest will complain, deter others and potentially defect.

Nothing good comes of bad customer experiences.

Making the Connection to Transparency.

How do you feel when someone lies to you?

There are probably variables depending on who it is and what the circumstances are, but it almost never makes you happy.

When a business partner tells us a lie and we find out, it makes us unhappy. Even somewhat meaningless lies tend to rub us the wrong way.

Politicians making false promises, brands overselling their products and girlfriends telling us "It isn't you; it's me" — life has this endless cycle of manipulation, lies and omissions that drive us as consumers and people to the edge of insanity.

We just want the truth.

While sometimes the truth won't solve the problem, most consumers would just prefer to know what the real situation is. Take an enterprise technology rollout, for example. You are the CIO and you have a Jan 1 deadline to get the new CRM solution implemented and in place. It is Christmas Eve and you are getting ready to hunker down for a day off when your phone rings and you find out the project just derailed. The project manager for your software provider tells you that due to some unforeseen circumstances the project will likely not be complete until Feb 1.

If I were the CIO, I want to know first and foremost, what are these unforeseen circumstances?

I guarantee you that the CIO knows that projects like this can run into delays and he or she may even be willing to work with the change, but "unforeseen circumstances" doesn't work. When an important deadline is going to be missed, they will want to know more.

Just put yourself in their shoes. What would you want to know?

Perhaps the real reason was the loss of an employee, a supplier delay or a cash flow issue due to slow paying customers. There are a plethora of reasons that a project can become delayed. Anyone in the world of business and technology know this.

But it comes back down to transparency.

Being vague is like telling a lie. You are leaving the person on the other end holding the bag for what didn't get done.

Think back to the example above. I bet you the CIO is accountable to some people in his organization. He is going to have to go back and tell them why the deadline was missed. Do you think he wants to go back and say "unforeseen circumstances?" Me either.

The best chance you have is to give the real reason no matter how silly it might be and hope that your honesty connects with their humanity. Perhaps they have been in a similar situation etc.

Customers Are Smart, Tell Them the Truth

In a world where consumers are more informed and connected than ever, does it even make sense to hold back information? While I know some businesses have to deal with regulation and required withholding of information, most businesses do not.

Remember Bluehost and its temporary denial of service that left about 20 percent of the Internet down? I understand that these kinds of things happen and so do most of the others who suffered from this temporary loss of service. What I can't get over is the decision not to give any of us information. Knowing that many of the customers that went without service were basically out of business for a period of time, the least we could have hoped for was some transparency.

In this day and age we as consumers are smart. We are also as humans often more compassionate than we are made out to be.

In the end I would always rather know what is going on even if the situation is worse than anticipated. Most people share this sentiment.

We are at a critical point where companies have the chance to separate themselves from the pack by delivering on what so many have failed to do in the past: Honesty.

SOURCES:

Convince and Convert
http://www.convinceandconvert.com/the-social-habit/42-percent-of-consumers-complaining-in-social-media-expect-60-minute-response-time

Mashable
http://mashable.com/2012/09/29/social-media-better-customer-service

Mashable
http://mashable.com/2013/10/02/facebook-workday

Statistic Brain
http://www.statisticbrain.com/facebook-statistics

Business2Community
http://www.business2community.com/customer-experience/customer-experience-important-advertising-infographic-0726258#0tk3uJPk4xdBXitQ.32

FOR SALES PROFESSIONALS, TIMES HAVE CHANGED

The days of long sales lunches are dwindling. That time is now better spent figuring out how to demonstrate return-on-investment for clients. Integration firm sales professionals reflect on how the process has evolved.

"Clients are more and more looking for results. With our lives, both professionally and personally, getting busier and busier, there is less time spent on relationship building, but that does not completely eliminate the power of establishing a good relationship. As the old adage goes, 'We buy from people we like.' However, we need to modernize this sentiment to include, 'We buy from people we like, and who can deliver results.' It is up to the account representatives to understand the needs and wants of the client and to provide a great experience throughout the sales process and beyond."
—Bill Craig, Business Development Manager, Logic Integration

"My first sales job was about lugging in projectors and doing demos. That doesn't happen anymore. We were dealing with facilities managers and it was usually an advocate or a friend. They didn't need all these approvals and there was less scrutiny on prices. Now it's all scrutinized. We call it insight selling and it's really focused on understanding who you're dealing with. It's important to have an advocate as a client but it's far more important to find the mobilizers within an organization." —Dale Bottcher, Western Region VP of Sales, AVI-SPL

"There appears to be an 'arms distance' approach from potential clients that has created a huge obstacle to becoming a business partner. Building the relationship is three times more difficult than it has ever been.
—Bruce Kaufmann, President & CEO, Human Circuit

"Things have changed, no question about it, especially as the client changes from facility to IT. The relationship becomes solidified when problems get solved. But lunch is still a requirement!" — Michael Boettcher, CEO, Advanced AV

"We have found that our customers break down into several different categories. We still have many customers that look to us as partners or having a relationship with them, long lunch type customers. But our biggest and best customers are the ones that we look at as partners, and as partners we work with them in a team fashion. The team usually consists of an engineer, sales associate, project manager and, of course, a great install team. I do agree that our business model is very rapidly moving away foreseeing a smaller group of relationship only customers. Our biggest base our partners in business, and our business is quality presentations." —Rod Andrewson, Manager of Engineering and Project Management Services, CCS Presentation Systems

"It's still 100-percent relationship based sales, but it's a different kind of relationship. You can't walk in there acting like Rico Suave and expect to win the sale." — *Bill Chamberlin, VP of Sales, Verrex Corporation*

MAKE MEETING CLIENT EXPECTATIONS AN ENTERPRISE-WIDE INITIATIVE
By Chris Miller

First things first. Communication is not limited to sales. Communication is a company function that runs across all departments and disciplines. In a transactional model, more emphasis is on the sales person; however, in a complex sale it is a company function. Company leaders must constantly assess and reassess the roles and responsibilities of their client engagement model based on the profiles of the clients and clearly express the approach to company employees and clients. The company then needs the most important ingredient to effect that change — buy-in from everyone.

In 1995, our company, Fairview-AFX, was awarded the RIT/USA Today Quality Cup award that focuses on quality improvements on products or services. Fairview-AFX was honored with the prestigious award for building a model of customer satisfaction that was recognized for its simplicity and internal metrics that substantiated change in client communication and overall satisfaction. The cornerstone of the program was the "Pledge of Accountability"— a client code of ethics that all employees signed. It was also given to all clients who were expected to hold the company employees accountable.

The 12 pledges focused on simple commitments that helped solidify the relationship with the client and build a solid trust factor between the client and the company. To confirm that the pledge was being enforced, employees sent out surveys to clients after specific client engagements. The responses were tracked, employees were informed of the good and bad feedback, and total transparency between the company and the client was achieved. Sales, profits, and services all improved. There were still on-going problems in deliverables but they were not buried or overlooked by the employee or the company and employees celebrated client satisfaction and project "victories."

Over the years, I've been told that the pledge has been quoted at graduation ceremonies, worship services, and used repeatedly by companies and organizations as a guide to how clients should be treated. Why? I can only assume because it is still relevant, resonates with both clients and employees, and the individual pledges withstand the test of time — regardless of the influences of the times.

Today, there are many more communication tools available to the integrator and the client than in 1995 and yet *the gap between client expectations and company deliverables is as wide (or wider) than ever*. Unfortunately, employees tend to hide behind the communication tools — voice mail and email. Many employees prefer to communicate via email rather than pick up the phone and address the client's questions or requests. While email is a documentable communication tool that often hits the mark and is available 24 hours a day, it is an impersonal tool that can be misinterpreted. It also limits the opportunity to deal with real time issues that the client obviously wants addressed.

Measuring Customer Engagement

The integrator has to ask the following questions of their staff:
- What are the clients' expectations today?
- Are the expectations universal across the enterprise or are they specific to a group or individual in the company?
- What instruments do you have in place to collect client feedback?
- Is the feedback generalized about your company or specific to a deliverable, sale, or service engagement?
- Do you know if your clients are distractors, passive or promoters?

You can learn more about survey metrics and measurements on the Internet. As the old business adage says, "You can't manage what you don't measure." Once you begin to collect data you will start to see a road map of where you need to adjust your deliverables and narrow the gap between expectation and client response.

Another thing you have to ask as an owner is, "Do I create an environment that allows all employees across the various disciplines and offices to share the opportunities that are coming by them with ownership? Will they be rewarded with praise or money? Reprimanded for going around their manager? Laughed at for an idea that isn't fully developed?"

In short, does your company culture reinforce client satisfaction and expectations?

Today, our network, Professional Network Systems International (PNSI), sends out "experience" surveys to clients throughout North America. The survey asks clients to rank their level of satisfaction with a specific integration or service experience. It is not a "How do you like our company?" survey. We do not focus on generalities, just specific interactions. The network is building a database and profile of what clients expect from an experience.

The results are confidential to the client and the integrator and the consolidated rankings are used to set benchmarks for integrators to meet or achieve. Setting benchmarks raises accountability and performance, often across nearly all employees who participated, and allows for developing better "best practices" that create lean deliverable systems that ultimately provide higher levels of client satisfaction and increased profits to the integrator or service provider.

What are the most common "open ended" comments that upset clients? You might be surprised. One of the most common complaints of clients regarding service and support is sending out technicians that are not equipped (technically capable as admitted by the technician) to fix or address the issue. Other top issues include not keeping the client informed of repairs and replacement parts. Clients note that they have to proactively call the integrator/service provider to find out status rather than posting the updated information online, email or by phone communication. Clients overall would like weekend and 24-hour support. All are opportunities to sell enhanced services that differentiate standard response and service and support at the level required by the client.

However, it is easy to offer services but delivering as promised is something different!

Communication Technology's Influence on Client Expectations

There is no doubt that we live in a time of immediacy. Today, expectations are higher than ever and clients expect prompt response and action at no additional cost to them. Why not? Clients do not always separate their expectations based on what they are buying. They want quick information, ability to order quickly, access to status and updates 24 hours a day, and want it to work as promised. Regardless.

Is too much information dangerous in the hands of the client?

Do we want to avoid transparency and accountability in our delivery systems?

Do we blame it on the Internet?

It's important that we understand the Internet and social media and the role it plays in client expectations and satisfaction—not to demonize or ignore it as it continues to have a trickle-down effect in our industry and business. Let's face it. The relationship model is changing. This isn't the first time in the past 40 years that there has been significant shift in client expectations and it won't be the last. **Today's innovative communication tools will be tomorrow's antiquated methodologies and we will need to reinvent our companies.** Owning a small business is not for the faint hearted.

In short, social media and all of its fall-out have created some level of buying and thought chaos. Chaos is your friend. Chaos makes opportunities but timing is everything!

Connecting with the customer is becoming more electronic — whether we like it or not. With more ways to connect with clients they have more ways to control the communication process. Some clients won't take inbound calls or appointments. They want to control the communication stream with your input and the knowledge they can capture through social media and broad Internet knowledge. We have moved from a model of "How do I find you?" (since they can control whether you find them or have access to them) to a model that is "How can you find me?" In short, how can I create a presence that drives people to me?

Unfortunately, the conclusions that they may reach about your company may not be the complete picture or prepare them to make the best decisions about your company and other solution providers. That's where the sales person, system designer or project manager is still so valuable to the equation. I always told our sales team that "if the client wants to do business with you then the price will work itself out in the negotiations." I believe it still to be true.

Today, it doesn't really matter whether it is a B-B model or a B-C model. In many cases, they are the same.

Effective Management in Today's Environment

Years ago a business mentor told me "new ideas and opportunities are coming at you or going by you all the time. What will separate you from others is your ability to recognize those ideas and take advantage of those opportunities."

The fact is that most owners, leaders, and managers have their heads down doing what it takes to stay in business every day and often don't look up to see those ideas and opportunities coming at them, thereby missing opportunities to implement programs that are best for their company. I've been there and it's true.

It's a hard business to generate cash, and pundits that write about change need to understand it is a lot easier to write about it than it is to do it. A small change in market approach and strategic company direction has rippling effects throughout the company that a business owner has to consider — which often leads to paralysis through analysis. With margins that are thin, one small mistake or miscalculation can ripple through the company and create an irreversible slide into bankruptcy.

Sometimes the opportunity makes sense but it's not the right time — in infrastructure, personnel, or financially.

My first business mentor out of college told me as I accepted my first business management position that "the vote is always taken when you aren't in the room"— referring to how others see you as part of their plan going forward — whether you are elevated in the company or fired for cause. Over the years, I have seen this played out in many ways with clients firing integrators and clients not hiring integrators based on their reputation without giving the company the chance to present their solution or recommendations. In short, others often speak on your behalf — good and bad.

What will they say?

The best owners, leaders, and managers get their heads out of the day-to-day minutia of running a business and discover how to be part of the conversation before it even occurs. What used to be called damage control is now called reputation management. Whatever you want to call it, someone needs to ensure the company isn't the last to know what is being said about them.

In the past, sales and marketing were using different tools, however, today they are starting to use the same tools. There are numbers floating that 60 to 70 percent of clients would rather hear how other clients feel about your company than what you tell them about your company.

Remember, the vote will be taken when you aren't in the room.

The client doesn't need to fully trust the Internet. However, the client has to "trust" the sales team or the company. It is important that companies fully understand the role of sales — it is trust and creativity. For the most part, social media can't diagnose and deliver a solution specific to each client's need. Social media and the Internet can't discern client behavior. Social media can help the client recognize business opportunity benefits but the decision will be made on knowledge, trust, and the potential to change the way they currently do business.

The service contract is the apparent holy grail of recurring revenue streams for integrators. The Internet (often the clients' primary business advisor) will suggest that service agreements are rip-offs and that the company is making 100 percent profit. Assume your clients are Googling "service agreements" and will come to these conclusions. In many cases the articles about service agreements are consumer products and are replacement-based insurance policies.

In the case of the systems integrator, however, most support agreements we provide are very different solution offerings. If the integrator team mistakenly calls the solution a "service contact" even though the actual line item is called something clever it will be assumed by the client that it is a scam not worth buying — and the level of trust between the client and the solution provider is compromised.

Yes, selling preventative or support agreements or managed service agreements can help shorten the response time to the client. In some cases it may include having full-time staff on the client's premises. However, if the team or individual promoting the maintenance or support agreement is selling something that can't be measured or delivered then the results will be catastrophic and the recurring aspect of the agreement will be eliminated and the client lost for all future business.

In summary, don't sell a service agreement just for the revenue if you don't have a model for deliverables. Over-committing and under-delivering is something we all hear about other integrators all the time.

What is the client saying about you and where are they saying it?

Chris Miller is executive director of Professional Systems Network International.

Chapter 4:
Value Lies In Your Creativity

THE ROLE OF CREATIVITY IN VALUE CREATION

Any business owner worth his salt knows he needs to create value if he wants to win and keep customers.

Unless you are playing in the commodity world where your price is the only value you offer, "value creation" really should be broken into two parts. First, let's dissect the that two-word term.

Value: What is a product, service or combination of the two worth to its consumer? This is most often reflected in monetary terms.

Creation: The act of creating something; in this case, creating value.

While there is nothing overly complicated about how these two words break down, there is a massive opportunity for interpretation here. The bottom line is value is in the eye of the beholder and it is up to the provider to "create" that value.

Creation as in Creativity

We have talked about the changing landscape for sales and how the informed consumer is uprooting the sales process, as we know it. So the question now becomes, "What do we do about it?"

One thing is for sure, we can't just sit back and let our customers walk out the door. However, if we aren't supplying them with value, that is exactly what they are going to do.

It comes down to creativity. Not just being creative for the sake of being creative; rather, becoming the *business partner* that brings value back to the partnership.

Think about the changing role this way. In the past, it was the role of the supplier to bring the customer from start to finish in the sales cycle.

When the customer would come to our door they were almost like children. They needed to be taught how to eat, how to dress and how to take care of themselves. Once they learned those things they became proficient and the focus shifted to teaching them the next thing.

Now they come to us and they are like a student that just graduated college, chock full of knowledge and barely a clue as to what to do with that knowledge.

This is where your "creative value" comes into play.

Your organization is now in the role of "real world mentor" and it is your responsibility to help them take the raw knowledge (data) that is in their head from all of that content they are consuming and to make something useful of it.

Value Creation Example

Let's say a customer comes to you and says, "I have been reading all about Web-based video conferencing solutions and I would like to explore implementing them into our business."

If doing business in the old way, you might respond by saying:

"Great, we sell Cisco Webex. It is a great product. Let me get you a quote, ok?"

In the new value creation focused world the response should

be a little bit different. Perhaps it would go something like this:

Client: I have read a lot about web based video conferencing and would like to explore further on how we can implement them here at Acme Corporation.

Vendor: Tell me more about which products you have read about. And more importantly, why do you believe it is a good solution?

Clients: Our organization is trying hard to allow our employees to be more mobile while also cutting back on some of our travel costs.

Vendor: There are several suppliers of this type of technology. You may or may not know of them. I'd love to help you get some test accounts set up and we can do some A/B/C user testing to see which solutions best fit your enterprise needs.

Clients: That would be great. It would also be great to get some use-based analytics of how the tools are being used, which devices they are being used on and whether people are enjoying the experience.

Vendor: Absolutely, we can do that. Let me put a test plan together and we will go from there.

What have we learned?

Maybe it doesn't stand out that the vendor did anything miraculous to create value, but the dialog reflects a shift in what consumers are seeking from their vendor and this is precisely the shift that creates value.

The client came to the vendor seeking two things:

- Validation of their idea/interest in a product (Web-based conferencing)
- Support in testing, analyzing, implementing and adoption

The first part reflects a more common business practice in relationship selling. In this case it's a need for analysis and validation.

The second part reflects a monumental shift in how businesses engage in adopting new technologies — a model known as "land and expand" (which will be covered in an upcoming chapter). In short, it's that what the customer is looking for is a partner that wants to help in the sales process because there are so many unknowns in the procurement of services that you become a partner in mitigating risk as well as delivering solutions.

By helping the customer vet a product you build trust and credibility, and if the process goes well you all but lock yourself in as the vendor of choice.

The risks are inherently higher because the sales process lengthens and there is a distinct possibility that the product or service won't catch on. But really it comes down to you as the partner providing the insight on which products they should try and then being aligned in the rollout, education and adoption process to make sure the solution does what it was intended.

Comes Down to Being Creative

In the end, it all comes down to creating value. Always ask yourself this question as you are working with clients:

What is our organization adding to the equation?

More importantly...

Does the client need me to successfully get from where they are to where they want to go?

In our example, just quoting and selling "Cisco Webex" makes that partner one of about 30,000 potential suitors in the United States. If your value is nothing more than being there at that moment then you have very little to stand on.

However, if you help that client take that baseline of knowledge and put it to use to deliver something that truly solves an organizational problem, you are making yourself invaluable.

This is precisely why being creative is at the center of delivering value and creating customer experience in a market place where the rules have changed.

How does your business add creativity to deliver better customer experience?

INFORMATION TO DRIVE INSPIRATION

The desire to pay attention to your customer is a noble one. In fact, I believe wholeheartedly that customer experience is the future of marketing. That is because it is only with our customers as ambassadors and a source of revenue that our businesses will thrive.

Having said that, what it means to pay attention to the customer has changed. Most notably the customer's needs from its providers have changed and therefore your business must change with it. What used to be the high-touch sales method of product overviews, long lunches and happy hours has shifted from the core of relationship selling to a mere side show.

These days, customers are seeking more and more of their own information on just about every product and service on the planet long before they even let their vendors know what they are looking for. With this a business must change from what relationship selling was to what it *is*.

New Approach to Relationship Selling

So with so much change in the customer landscape, what makes a business partner valuable today?

To make it as simple as possible I have created two buckets where businesses should focus their customer engagement:

Information: Like I've said many times before, consumers are seeking out information on their own. As a vendor, you should seek to become a supplier of valuable and practical information that helps drive your customers toward a purchase decision. If you aren't the source of information, it may be a good idea to ask yourself who is. Chances are it is another supplier, which is the last place you want your clients to be gathering their information.

How can you become a source for information? This is where creating and curating copious amounts of useful information on how your products and services solve real business problems comes into play. Creating is quite literally the act of having marketing and leadership write, record video and use graphical data to help your customer better understand your solutions. Curating means finding valuable sources and pointing your customers toward it via email, social media or other correspondence.

Inspiration: This is the part where suppliers can really set themselves apart. How do you inspire action from your current and potential customers? It's not just about getting them to buy, but about moving them forward in the process and creating a vision around the value your solutions provide. If the customer is truly informed (they are) and they think they know what they want (they do), how do you take that and help guide them toward maximizing the data (information) that they have consumed?

Think about this from a practical perspective. People now love to do their own research. They think they know exactly what they want. As a solution provider, it is on you to ask questions, listen, check the facts and ultimately to make sure what they think they know is valid. Then it's on you to ensure that they get what they really want, not just what they *think* they want.

In the end, your business exists because you bring value. The moment you stop adding value you will be commoditized or worse yet you will cease to exist.

Focus on being the source of information *and* inspiration for your customers (old and new). This isn't just what they want, but it is what they *need* from their suppliers.

Is your business customer centric? How do you inform and inspire your customers to assure successful outcomes?

CONVERTING KNOWLEDGE

Did you know that the average organization allows its employees to dedicate less than 10 percent of their time to foster ideas of innovation?

That means today's knowledge worker isn't being put to use to drive innovation, but rather to fulfill and support the business that is already there.

The word "innovation" may immediately make you think of technologists, developers and engineers; however, the number above is all encompassing and includes areas of innovation like business process improvement, customer service improvement and employee satisfaction innovation.

Innovation while often only thought of as emerging technology is really the process of making *anything* better. This includes making better businesses.

So what makes the perfect vendor? Put another, less subjective way, what company in their right mind would kick a vendor to the curb that is helping them improve their business?

With so little time being spent on innovation, there is an opportunity for your company to truly differentiate by helping your clients innovate. Doing this requires a few things, but nothing that we can't do if we paid mind to it. These focuses would be on customer's needs, emerging trends, adoption and application and, of course, continuous improvement.

Customer Needs: We discussed the importance of anticipating what your customers need. This comes down to selling the invisible or shedding light on something that may not be obvious to your clients at this time.

Remember the statistic about 70 percent of the sales process being complete prior to the customer engaging a vendor? Getting out in front of your customer needs allows you to circumvent the late entry into the process. By helping customers to gain clarity in where their business needs are moving you have put yourself at the forefront of the sale and brought yourself into the early phases of the sale.

One important factor in successfully identifying customer needs is keeping your eyes on where your industry is moving, which brings us to the next point.

Emerging Trends: Every industry has internal and external forces that are driving change. Regardless of what business you

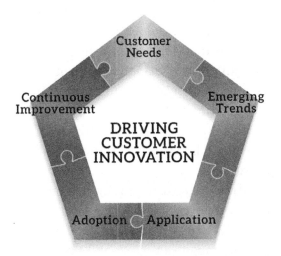

are in, movement is happening and to be a catalyst of innovation for your customers you need to be close to those changes.

To do this you need to constantly ask yourself the following questions:

- What are the biggest changes in our business in the past 5 years, 1 year, 6 months?
- What do these changes tell me about what trends are coming up next?
- Are the trends cyclical or are they linear?*
- How will these changes affect our clients and what can our product or services do to allow these changes to be a positive force for change within their businesses?

*Think of linear change as a trend that is going to continue to change with no foreseeable reversal (e.g., the price of hard disk storage), whereas a cyclical change or trend is something that may have an impact on business but could and likely will reverse at some point (e.g., real estate or fashion).

Application: Once you have helped your client determine their need, one of the areas that businesses struggle the most is identifying how the solution can be applied to their business.

To "theoretically" inspire someone is one thing, but to help them envision and apply it to their operation is another story. Many businesses do a terrific job of selling the customer on the need, but they fall flat on their face in the application phase.

In the presentation system integration business, where I have spent the vast majority of my career, there is a widely recognized 95 percent rule, which reflects how the majority of integrators struggle to complete a project and they usually get stuck in the last 5 percent. I have seen it as a consumer as well with enterprise software and hardware deployments. I have been sold on CRM packages, ERP solutions and data center configurations that are supposed to work one way but almost always come up just short.

So while helping your customer see the value of the application is the first major step to adding value, the second part is making sure the implementation is successful and the expected adopted rates are reached quickly and painlessly.

Adoption: If you identify the trends, assess the needs, determine the application and fail to gain adoption, you will fall flat on your face.

In the past I referred to how video conferencing was an idea that never reached its potential. This is where application versus adoption becomes glaringly obvious. When video conferencing was first introduced, many of the manufacturers and resellers wanted to sell the enterprise on how video would save them money, specifically travel and business expense.

Where the manufacturers missed the mark was that the users didn't want to stop traveling and visiting their clients. Video was more useful to augment real life interaction not to replace it. With the technology early on being hard to use, people found any reason they could to continue doing business the old way and were resistant to adopting the new technology.

As video and collaboration platforms have become more affordable adoption has been easier. However, to this day many organizations only *augment* their travel with video, as it has never truly been a replacement for real life engagement.

In the future adoption is and will continue to be key to being seen as value added or differentiated as organizations will continue to need to improve the expediency by which new products, services and ideas are adopted.

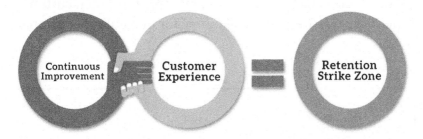

Continuous Improvement: The final driver for supporting client innovation is an organization's contribution to the continuous improvement of use and the aforementioned adoption of the products and/or services supplied.

In short, rapid proliferation is shortening the product life-cycle of just about everything a business consumes. However, when you help an organization to maximize their investments you are aiding their ability to innovate. This can be finding ways they can more strategically allocate funds or ways they can integrate new solutions into their existing.

One industry that does this very well is the cloud CRM

industry. Salesforce, the market leader offers an Application Exchange where users can further expand the capabilities of their investment in Salesforce by bolting on best of breed applications for supply-chain, social listening, finance and other business process automation areas.

This type of flexible innovation allows the users of Salesforce to maximize their investment in the platform. This also builds interdependence between salesforce users and the solution making the likelihood of defection very low since so much of a user's business is on the platform.

Make no mistake. SaaS vendors like SalesForce and others do this on purpose to hook their customers in on the solution.

When a strategy has your business tightly integrated to your client business and you focus on providing top-notch customer experience you are in the strike zone for unparalleled customer retention.

SOURCES:

Intrepid Learning
http://intrepidlearning.com/blog/how-companies-spur-innovation-infographics

CREATIVE SELLING – WHAT IT REALLY MEANS

We can all agree that creative thinking can benefit most profession-als, but how does creativity manifest itself when it comes to selling? We asked integration firm executives to weight in:

"Ten years ago if I wanted to listen to a song, I would go buy the CD and listen in my car or home and enjoy the music. It was easy. Today, if I want to listen to that same song, I can still go buy the CD (if I can find a store that sells CDs), buy it online from iTunes or Amazon or Napster, or stream it online through Spotify, Pandora, I Heart Radio, Amazon Cloud, Sirius XM or a dozen other options.

"The same scenario goes for watching a movie with iTunes, Amazon, Hulu, Netflix, Roku, and traditional disk technologies. These examples are dealing with the sim-plest of tasks of listening to music or viewing a movie. The complexity level raises exponentially when we start dis-cussing distributed audio, distributed video, digital projec-tion, networked systems, automated systems, integrated building technology and list goes on and on.

"The growth of technology options is both liberating, and crippling for our customers. Now, more than ever, it is the job of the account reps to completely understand the client needs, help the client navigate the sea of solutions, and direct them to the right technology solution.

"Sometimes that requires creativity but a lot of times it requires understanding the client needs and simplifying the technology options down to the best option for that specific project." —Bill Craig, Business Development Manager, Logic Integration

"I can't even begin to quantify the extent to which sales people need to be creative. The natural distrust of sales associates is at an all-time high because of the information and often misinformation provided through the Internet."
—Bruce Kaufmann, President & CEO, Human Circuit

"The challenge from clients to integrators is to 'solve my problem ... one I might not even know I have yet.' [Sales people can share] success stories of similar organizations, samples of usage, identifying obstacles and providing a team of support have become the basis of selling today. Leave the power point at home." —Michael Boettcher, CEO, Advanced AV

"It's everything from looking to create a relationship with a client to creating one long term. It's not just about somebody being smart on the technology side but really understanding the business, and really understanding the client's unique strategies." —Bill Chamberlin, VP of Sales, Verrex Corporation

"The last three years we have become extremely creative in the ways that we try to help our customers arrive at the solutions that they need to support their presentation needs. We built a showcase facility built by us and outfitted by our manufacturing partners, projector, speaker, control system, VTC, electronic whiteboard, anything AV presentation oriented you can imagine in one group of rooms. Then we invite groups based on the types of vertical markets a specific sales associates may be working with, [for example] K-12, to an after-hours networking party where they can meet our engineers, installers, manufacturing partners and

see equipment in a working real-world environment.
"This is been extremely successful. We also put together a
national summit. We put the summit on every other year and
invite all of our national offices, a select group of our manu-
facturing partners, and VIP customer partners. The venue for
the event is a local four-star resort and conference Center.
There is a trade show floor for the manufacturing partners to
display their goods. We also provide professional continuing
education in the AV industry as well as topics that are perti-
nent to successful business for our national offices. This last
year we had over 400 people attend a special concert that we
provided with Crystal Gayle as the entertainment. This was
a lot of fun and very successful for everyone who attended."
*—**Rod Andrewson, Manager of Engineering and Project***
Management Services, CCS Presentation Systems

CREATIVE SELLING IN AV (OR ANY INDUSTRY) - BOON OR BS?
By K.C. Schwarz

Let's start with the beginning: Selling is life! Have you ever seen a three-year-old "sell" her version of a visit to the park or a teenager "sell" his version of a weekend with the car keys? Sure you have!

We are *born* to sell those things that inspire us with passion, no matter how ultraistic or misguided. Why is it that, as AV professionals, we bury our passion and lose our mojo? We become stiff; we list abstract features; and we fail to connect. I may not have the ultimate answers, but herewith let me provide some (slightly biased!) observations that may shed light on this dilemma.

In the first place, make no mistake, selling is difficult. Why? Because, unlike childhood or adolescent selling which is based on self-interest, selling as a profession is based on a total reversal — assuming the other's interest. This is quite a switch in our "me-centric" world. The first step in creative selling is to get outside of yourself and look at the world through your customer's eyes.

So, let's connect the dots: A teenager is creative in selling his dad on a weekend with the car keys because he wants to make an impression. Your customer wants and AV system because she wants to make an impression. Do you know what it is and why? If the campus facilities director at your local community college is asking about a digital signage wayfinding system, get creative! Invite her to lunch twice — once with a focus group of satisfied customers from your reference high school and once with a focus group of "directionally challenged students" from her college. Help her feel the difference; it's no fun to be lost and late!

Next, from your customer's eyes, survey the landscape. On the technology front "AV guys" have a huge advantage: Human eyes and ears will always, *always* be analog. The IT world is entirely digital. AV controls the "last 18 inches" to human cognition — eyes and ears. What does your customer want to see and hear? That's real AV. So, the first rule is to listen to and inspire a vision of your customer's ultimate AV experience.

To inspire your customers, listen to their hopes and dreams, and define what's possible. Paint an image of AV greatness. To do this, you must know what is possible, at every level. But remember, it's about creating an emotional landscape, not selling hardware.

Now to the heart of the matter — sell the system. Anybody can deliver parts. It's our job to envision, create, sell and deliver the system. Systems engineering was one of the greatest accomplishments of the 20th century. We created a system to put men on the moon. Out of this discipline we are able to deliver unbelievable experiences.

Are you excited about your team's ability to engineer and deliver systems that embody AV greatness?

Do you change the game in a corporate boardroom?

Do the schools you serve produce smarter students?

Does that church project you sold reach the flock in awesome ways?

Be sure not to be caught in the "low cost trap. What's that? Cost is absolute and value is relative.

Move the value bar above the cost bar. To do this you must wear a consultant's hat and ask consultative questions. The leading question is, "Can you explain why you want to ...?"

As a consultant you are responsible for providing a valuable solution. o do this you must understand your customer's value proposition. Your ears are your most valuable selling tool, not your mouth!

Because of its personal nature, we must be willing to demonstrate the value of AV, in advance. Words can't describe the full reach and depth of a transformative AV experience. I remember vividly my first surround-sound movie experience, *The Battle of Midway* in 1976. That was an "audio epiphany!" If you can't afford a full blown demo environment, find a supportive customer and commit to a fantastic AV project at no margin if they will let you use there system as a demo environment, on occasion and with permission. You may be surprised at their willingness to share the limelight!

Finally, be prepared to commit to and deliver quantifiable results. As an AV professional, your responsibility is to communicate, sell, and deliver a "wow" experience. You know (or should know) the technical metrics and specifications that make exceptional AV experiences a reality. In this role you are the "interpreter" between your customer and the design/engineering elements of you team. Comprehend your customers' dreams and work with your engineering team to make them a reality!

Walt Disney said, "All our dreams can come true, if we have the courage to pursue them." Have the courage to sell by listening to your customers' dreams and delivering AV experiences that inspire!

K.C. Schwarz is CEO of USAV Group.

Chapter 5:
The Role of the Human Network

Would you be the least bit surprised if I told you that 98 percent of businesses depend almost entirely on word of mouth marketing?

What if I told you that of those 98 percent, only 3 percent have a strategy for obtaining leads via word-of-mouth?

Here is my reaction to that: SCARY!

If your No. 1 way of obtaining new business isn't even something you have a strategy for, it's time to rethink what you are doing.

The good news is networking has become easier to do than ever.

According to my LinkedIn profile where I have just over 1,900 first-degree connections, I am within two degrees of nearly 18,000,000 professionals.

This means that between myself, and my friends and *their* friends, I have access to a whole lot of people. This is really powerful.

Our Networks Are Becoming Our Biggest Influencers.

Think about the last time you were making a major purchase decision or hiring somebody. Where did you go to seek advice? You probably sought insight from the Internet.

For your purchase you may have begun by searching Google

for trusted sources where you could research and become better versed in whatever it was you were buying, say a house, a car or a major appliance.

As for a hiring decision, did you reach out to your professional network? Perhaps post a note on your LinkedIn Network or pick up the phone and call a few friends that you thought may have some intimate knowledge of a few perfect candidates?

ONLINE SERVICES MOST LIKELY TO INFLUENCE A PURCHASE

Retail Sites	56%
Brand Sites	34%
Blogs	31.1%
Facebook	30.8%
Groups/Forums	28%
YouTube	27%
LinkedIn	27%
Google+	20%
Online Magazines	20%
Pinterest	12%
Twitter	8%
News Sites	7%
Instagram	3%

If this sounds at all like the way you consume, then you aren't in the minority. Considering 92 percent of all companies use Social Media as a top vehicle for hiring, I would say that you are in the majority.

Consumers 35 years and younger, which is a rapidly growing portion of management in the workforce, are 50 percent more likely to make a buying decision based on a recommendation they received through their social network.

Another emerging trend is that blogs and social networks are quickly becoming the "de facto" source of inspiration for purchasing decisions. If you omit the impact of retail sites, which are primarily a vehicle for B2C, blogs and social media as the key influencers in purchase decisions are quickly surpassing brand sites.

Why Are a Businesses Networks So Influential For Customer Engagement?

Networks reach far beyond just social, although it is more common than not that people connect to their "in person" networks via social media networks, making the two somewhat ubiquitous.

By default, we trust people that we are close with and for some reason we also show more implicit trust to the brands that we follow. In fact, 64 percent of consumers are more likely to buy from a brand they follow on Twitter, demonstrating that we become more emotionally connected to the brands we are engaged with.

For businesses that stay closely aligned with their customers this provides a massive advantage. With the ubiquitous nature of social networking along with the high-touch capabilities that most B2Bs have, the opportunities to stay close to customers and to build trust are tremendous.

The best thing is that social vehicles provide an opportunity for companies to connect more frequently in less intrusive fashions, providing a win-win for the customer and the provider.

Back To Your Word of Mouth Strategy

The statistics alone make it pretty overwhelmingly clear that a business' network is pivotal to its ongoing growth potential.

The trend toward doing our own research (see Chapter 2)

and looking to our friends for guidance in purchase decisions are trends that are only going to continue to proliferate. Knowing that our personal business activities are becoming more ubiquitous with our professional business activities makes this more evident than ever.

So businesses cannot ignore the importance of building a network. This includes the business being high-touch through low-touch mediums like social, email and other education opportunities.

It also is dependent on businesses having a strategy to maximize the networks of its employees.

While there is much uncertainty about what an organization can ask for when it comes to their employees' social media activities, **there is absolutely nothing wrong with an organization asking its employees to engage their personal and professional networks in a way that is valuable to all parties involved.**

Successful selling has always had a certain prerequisite of asking for a sale in order to earn it. The big change today is that the asking is much less direct.

The positive is our reach to current and potential customers is better than ever and leveraging those relationships is one of the most important tactics in growing leads and converting business in the connected economy.

BUILDING A MORE MEANINGFUL NETWORK

(Through Enablement, Content and Customer Activation)
If your company is among the 98 percent that depend heavily on word of mouth marketing to drive new business, perhaps it is time to consider your network to be your best friend?

No matter how robust the network is that you have built, there is always an opportunity to further expand your reach to drive new and exciting opportunities into your business. If networking has never been your thing, then now is the absolute best time to work on getting that network in shape because you will never have the luxury of knowing that you need a strong network until the moment that you do.

That is exactly why your business and your team need to focus on building a highly connected organization that drives high levels of ongoing engagement across both online and offline platforms.

Begging the question ... How does an ordinary organization become extraordinarily connected?

By "connected" I mean your direct connections, whether you are in sales, marketing, executive leadership or other, and I mean your brand evangelists which are fans, followers and other more passively engaged to you and your company. Both are important and need to be focused on and nurtured to build a more social and connected organization.

Building a connected organization comes down to three major factors that start at the top of the organization and works its way down.

Factor 1: Enable and Exemplify

The most successful organizations at building a strong connected brand tend to have leaders that are enablers. Beyond just enabling their employees to focus on building their networks, often the leaders themselves are highly connected. Senior management should first lead by example. This includes being active on professional networking sites like LinkedIn, but also being local in their business community by joining leadership groups like Young Presidents (YPO), Vistage, YEC

(Young Executives Council) and other similar organizations throughout their communities.

Another avenue of increasing connections is for the organizational leaders to join industry trade associations where they can take leadership roles and influence the future direction of their industry.

In my experience, anytime I have worked with an organization where the leaders were "hermit crabs," that type of non-connectedness tended to proliferate throughout the organization. Leaders that enable and exemplify the importance of connectedness tend to build the most meaningful networks.

Factor 2: Content Driven:

In today's high paced society it is extremely hard to be noticed when you are just reaching out asking people to notice you. Now more than ever we are in a world gone viral where people are constantly turning their heads in the direction of the next shiny thing. Therefore, **merely showing up is no longer good enough for building a network.**

What people look for is value in every connection and while we hate to make human relationships seem even the least bit transactional, there is just a little bit (or a lot) of what can you do for me in every connection.

Consider This: How do you connect to others? When do you choose to accept an invitation on a social platform like LinkedIn? Are you selective or open? Remember these things when you are building your network.

With the more selective nature by which people (especially

decision makers) are making connection decisions, the question comes down to how is your organization arming itself to influence and inspire people to follow, like and connect with your brand and team members?

The secret weapon for driving connected organizations comes down to content. And not just any content, but target rich, high-quality engaging content that decision makers would want to read.

What Does Target Rich, High Quality, Engaging Content Look Like?

For a business that wants to build its network, both direct content as well as fans and followers online, you need to focus on delivering value through your content.

Hence the *Target Rich, High Quality and Engaging* comment.

You and I both know those make for great buzzwords, but what does that really mean and how does your organization put out this type of content across paid, owned and earned platforms.

Paid: Websites where you pay for your content to be featured. (e.g. Adwords or other PPC marketing)
Owned: Web properties and social bookmarks that you own. (e.g. Your website, Facebook page, LinkedIn page)
Earned: When others share your content or publish it on their sites.

Here is a rundown of how you should create content to build your direct network and grow your loyal brand advocates.

Quality: Whether your company is creating the content or

curating content from others, make sure the information comes from reliable sources and is of a pre-determined quality standard (high). You never want people to read the information you are sharing and see it as low quality or spammy in its nature.

Useful: Create, curate and share content that delivers useful information on your products, services and marketplace to customers (current and prospective).

Engaging: When promoting content to your network, how are you framing what you are sharing so readers feel the inclination not just to consume, but respond. This can include passive engagement like having them re-share your content across their owned sites or it can be a more active engagement like having them comment, subscribe or sign up for more. Engagement is the key to converting prospects into customers and current customers into more invested customers.

Once you have the content at your disposal, the next key is getting it in front of people in a "soft sale" manner.

Think of it this way: Would you rather get a handwritten letter in the mail or a mass email that shows up as spam?

The way you seek to receive information should be a key in determining your strategy in delivering content to others.

While most companies will (and should) use some type of mass delivery to its mail list, one of the best ways to drive engagement with content is for your sales and executives to utilize content to create a brief customer message to a target audience.

Say your organization conducts a case study on how your new software can save them 25 percent annually on their data storage expense.

What if you took 5 minutes to write a note to 3, 4 or 5 targeted individuals in your network whom you have discussed a similar topic with? It could read:

"Hi Ms. Customer,
How is it going? We just completed this interesting case study
on how clients can significantly save money with our new soft-
ware. I remember we talked about how you were looking to
decrease costs on your data storage and that is exactly what our
software will do.
I hope you find this helpful. Let me know if I can answer any
other questions otherwise I will reach out in a few days to fur-
ther discuss.
Sincerely,
Todd Smith, YourCo Software"

Simple, targeted and useful.

If you had indeed discussed this topic I would be willing to
bet the prospect would be really grateful that you took the time
to reach out. Now have your entire team do this a couple of
times a week and you are building an army of loyal, engaged
prospects that should keep your pipeline healthy for the foreseeable future.

This brings us to the final factor.

Factor 3: Customer Activated Organization

Even the most connected organization with the best content on
the planet will fail if they get the third factor wrong.

Organizations that want to prosper in the new economy
must be customer activated. This means they show clearly,
without question, that they are customer focused.

With bad service experience being the No. 1 driver of defection (68 percent), organizations must continuously and rigor-
ously show their network that they are customer driven.

Perhaps you are thinking, what does this have to do with building a customer-focused organization?

If you recall, the purpose of a strong business network is to drive word of mouth. For a company focused on growing, word of mouth marketing is key and will come directly from your network.

Therefore, to grow a network, *rather than churn a network,* an organization must be focused on creating positive customer experiences.

While most certainly an overarching factor that drives more than just your businesses network, any business looking to improve its referral business knows that the easiest way to drive referral business is to have happy customers that are going to say great things about your business.

As a litmus test I recommend you go through your top clients (80/20) and ask yourselves if you would use each client as a reference. Ideally, the answer should be yes to all of them.

It's About Leadership, Information and Customer Focus

In the end building a strong personal, professional and organizational network comes down to having a culture that embraces networking, providing a constant drip of quality information to your audience and having a relentless focus on delivering high levels of customer satisfaction.

If you were to evaluate your business in these three areas, would it make the grade?

BUILDING YOUR ONLINE BRAND: A SMALL BUSINESS DIGITAL STRATEGY GUIDE

Perhaps the most asked question of small businesses in the past three years is, "How do we measure return on social media,

<u>blogging</u> and <u>digital marketing</u>?"

Translation: If we spend time, money or energy on these pseudo marketing activities, is there a measurable return we can expect (in like five minutes)?

Since we are impatient for ROI on **digital marketing**, let me ask you another question: Does every ongoing conversation that you have with your customers translate to a measurable return? You know, those golf outings, happy hours, incentive trips and other glad-handing activities. Can you truly calculate revenue to your bottom line from those relationship-building activities?

Of course not. Yet, we do them anyhow.

When you answer the question completely honestly, the bottom line is you just don't know. You think you know because customers may tell you they had a terrific time, but unless you are in a controlled experiment where you can hold the "relationship building" variable constant, there is no actual way of knowing.

Relationship Building, Done Online

If I had to liken *digital marketing* to something that makes sense for any business person on the planet, it would be this: **The way your company does digital marketing should be exactly like the way it does "real life" relationship building.**

With this caveat, the assumption is your business cares about nurturing customers, suppliers and relationships. So what does this mean? You can't golf, have dinner or share a cocktail over Wi-Fi, so it isn't exactly the same.

But what you can do is be consistently engaging, provide **content** that is high-quality and useful to your prospective and current clients, and make sure to be responsive in a similar manner to traditional mediums.

It is through those recurring and valuable interactions that relationships between buyers and brands take place, making your brand more humanistic and the relationship more meaningful.

Is Online Engagement the New SEO?

Did you know that Google is changing its algorithm yet again to make it impossible for marketers to see what keywords are driving search traffic to their site?

Yup, it completely changes the game and simultaneously puts the onus back on companies to actually talk to their customers. I liken this to how old media advertising has lost tremendous value as people stop reading physical newspapers and how they now skip commercials with their DVRs.

Freedom of choice allows people to choose what *content* they engage with. Much like who we befriend, buyers now engage with brands and content they want, and the ability for marketers to short circuit this with adwords and other keyword marketing techniques is being trivialized more and more each day.

Should Marketing Trump Sales?

Companies spend more on sales and pay their sales people more. This isn't subjective; it is absolute truth. Companies often see sales as paramount to marketing. Some companies don't market at all, they really just depend on sales to go find customers and it can work to an extent.

But today things are changing. According to Forrester, potential buyers are more than 70 percent through the purchasing decision before they engage sales.

If this is the case, where are they getting their info from? Clearly not from a sales person.

They are getting it from content marketing. Moreover, they are reading the blogs and other content shared by companies and using that as the insight they need to move toward a purchase decision.

The same report indicated that the amount of content a buyer engaged with prior to a purchase was 10 pieces in 2011, up from five in 2010. Hence, people are getting more dependent on content for buying decisions, technology amongst the highest in dependency.

So spend away on sales, but the impact may be less than you think.

Final Word on Digital Marketing for Small Businesses

If you want your organization to have a strong online community, you have to treat digital marketing with the same care you treat your real life interactions. Behind the monitor are people at every end, and while the correspondences may at times feel less than human, they are.

But the winds of change are blowing and like the shift we have seen from hardware to integration and then integration to service, the way we communicate with customers is forever changed.

It is your choice whether to make that for the worse or for the better, but it is manageable. Is your company ready to take advantage of the new digital consumer?

What do you see as the future of digital marketing?

SOURCES:

The Guardian
*http://www.theguardian.com/small-business-network/2013/nov/27/
targeted-networking-social-media-business*

Social Media Examiner
*http://www.socialmediaexaminer.com/blogs-outrank-social-networks-
for-consumer-influence-new-research*

Lexology
*http://www.lexology.com/library/detail.aspx?g=57195a7e-e298-4e25-
b1be-3a41a446b9df*

Social News Daily
http://socialnewsdaily.com/9243/social-media-influence-on-our-lives

NETWORKING OVERTAKES ADVERTISING

People, by in large, are not influenced by advertisements. In fact there isn't a single "true" advertising medium that is trusted at a rate of greater than 50 percent.

In a world gone social we are influenced by our trusted network at a rate of near 90 percent, and that alone speaks volumes for where things are heading. While content marketing is really not new, it's finally hitting the radars of just about every CMO with a pulse.

Recognizing that content is far more trusted than ads with retail sites, brand sites and blogs being the three most influential content vehicles, brands are going to be looking at a way to move spend from lesser performing vehicles like advertising to greater performing methods like blogging, video and infographics.

Currently, brands are seeing the greatest results in building trust and community through their content efforts; however, their spend still goes more toward advertising.

To be precise, in 2013 nearly 50 percent of brands' social marketing spend goes to Facebook advertising and less than 10 percent went to influencer outreach and blogging. That means that brands spent 5x as much on Facebook ads as they did on creating owned content and driving earned media.

Think about it from your company's perspective. What are you more likely to trust and engage with — a Facebook ad or a blog post written by someone influential about the product or service?

What is even more crazy is that these out-of-proportion spends on advertising were after a 40 percent increase in what companies budgeted for social media in 2013. I believe this is leading us to a seismic shift in how brands will do business.

With Facebook making it harder for brands to be seen (even

paid brands) and the fact that sound "owned, earned" strategies will lead readers to brand owned sites, companies that want to drive influence going forward are going to have to focus on their influencer outreach.

To accomplish this, brands are going to need to seek out thought leaders and content creators that influence buying behavior in their respective industries.

Who Are These Thought Leaders?

While "thought leader" and "content creator" sound like fancy monikers, what I'm really talking about here are bloggers, represented by those who write and publish content to the web, most often on their own sites or on a multitude of their own sites.

While brands are enamored with vehicles like Facebook and Twitter to cultivate followers and drive brand engagement, the most influential people are merely using social channels to drive readers back to their sites (86 percent). This means that those that can influence their brands aren't well represented where the brands are looking for them, making it harder for brands to find influencers that can support their marketing initiatives.

While every brand's goals for marketing are a little bit different, I think it's safe to say that all brands have a goal to drive positive brand sentiment. This positive feeling toward a brand moves buyers' confidence level in making brand purchases higher as they see people they trust supporting a certain product or service.

For many companies that know their target audience, this makes influencer marketing even more valuable. This is because 54 percent of consumers believe a small highly engaged community is far more influential than a larger less loyal community. In fact, only 12 percent believe a larger community is more influential.

This data point is incredibly important and in actuality is very good news for brands looking to "buy influence."

In short, brands need to seek out influencers that can drive and create very small yet loyal communities to advocate for their brand.

With so many people through social channels being separated by only 1 or 2 degrees, a small yet highly loyal group can reach far and be much more compelling than a large army of wishy-washy folks who like a brand on Facebook or follow a brand on Twitter.

With buyers being influenced at far greater rates by people within their networks, brands are going to want to figure out how to get closer to the influencer.

Again, for each product and service the influencer may vary, but the data does not lie. People will buy from brands they trust and the trust comes squarely from content generated by the brands intention and unintentional community.

Going forward, influence will be the great brand equalizer, begging the question...

How will your brand use influence and outreach to turn those new to your brand into enthusiasts, and those that know your brand into ambassadors?

TO BE SOCIAL, OR ANTI-SOCIAL?
By Chuck Wilson

I believe the use of social media is one aspect to staying in touch with clients. I would categorize it as a small piece of the engagement puzzle. I caution people all the time that social media isn't a replacement for face-to-face, or one-on-one conversations. Yet, we see this happening all the time.

In an effort to utilize social media we run the risk of becoming less social and, in turn, having less social skills. We have to manage this accordingly.

In my opinion, social media is an add-on to the sales strategy, not a substitute for making contact with a client. Especially in our millennial workforce we see a group of people who, for whatever reason, is far more comfortable typing a message than speaking on the phone. They would rather make a You Tube video on their iPad than give a presentation to a room of people.

To me, customer engagement is about a blend of media, technology and personal interaction. As business owners and leaders we have to start with how this fits into an overall company culture perspective and clearly communicate with the sales team on how the company expects social media to be a part of the engagement picture.

Some companies pull this off really well, other don't.

Being adaptable on an individual client basis is increasingly important. Many clients are requesting the usage of social technologies to stay more current and updated on what's new and exciting. That really opens up the door to possibilities and the integrators who are well prepared have the advantage. On the other hand, I've seen the overuse of social media create exposure that quickly eroded the relationship.

One question I get repeatedly is: When a sales associate quits the company, do their social media contacts leave with them?

They sure do and where does that leave the business owner? I advise our members to assume this is going to happen at some point and build in safeguards to back up those contacts and have more than one person involved in the social strategy of your company.

If you put all your time and energy into a social media marketing campaign it can walk out the door. If you do nothing, you get left behind. Like most things doing social media in moderation is likely the best answer. I also wouldn't expect an immediate ROI on your social media investment as measured in sales.

Can social media improve customer engagement?

YES. Especially effective are short video clips when announcing new people, new products, new services, etc. A message from the CEO is an outstanding way to convey the value proposition, the vision, mission and ethics of your company.

I wouldn't bombard the customers with these but perhaps a monthly video announcement would be a great way to make sure they are keeping up with any changes happening at your business.

Balance is the key, use social media but don't become overly dependent on it. If you reply on social media exclusively to launch a new product or service, be prepared for disappointing results. If you use it to supplement the primary marketing strategy, you will be much better off.

It's just one important tool in the toolkit, not the only one.

Chuck Wilson is executive director of National Systems Contractors Association.

HOW B2B INTEGRATORS VIEW SOCIAL MEDIA

We can all agree that creative thinking can benefit most profession-als, but how does creativity manifest itself when it comes to selling? We asked integration firm executives to weight in:

"I am professionally active on LinkedIn, and personally ac-tive on other social media outlets. I keep my professional LinkedIn account up to date with achievements, experi-ence, trainings, and look out for new connections. After I meet with a client I will reach out and connect with them on LinkedIn. I do believe it is important for a business and sales associates to be connected via these tools.

"However, I have yet to get a lead or prospect from social networking. Not that this isn't possible and that the right person couldn't use this as an excellent resource for business development, I just have not seen it personally. I think that tools like LinkedIn will continue to grow in importance and could be used in the future as a modern-ized White Pages type resource to find professionals or business services.

I have always subscribed to the heart that Keith Fer-razzi puts behind connecting with others. It isn't just about have the most social network 'friends;' it is about how you truly connect and look out for those connections, as he states, 'you are not networking. You are connecting — sharing your knowledge, resources, time, energy, friends, associates, empathy and compassion in a continual effort to provide value to others. Real networking is about find-ing ways to make other people more successful.'

*"If we can use tools like LinkedIn in this manner, than I think they can be successful resources to develop business. But that takes time, dedication, and a true integrity to not have a what's in it for me attitude." —**Bill Craig, Business Development Manager, Logic Integration***

*Leveraging social media is "more important than ever. The social connections are serving to get personal introductions to decision makers which can at least provide a better platform to creating a solid relationship early." —**Bruce Kaufmann, President & CEO, Human Circuit***

*Social media is "almost as important as a referral today. This is usually a first step in business development. Whether we like it or not, this is where activity is taking place, and can help get you in the door if you work it right." —**Michael Boettcher, CEO, Advanced AV***

*"We love and are heavy users of social networking at CCS, but we've also found that good old-fashioned face-to-face networking is just a successful or more so. All of our executive leadership is tasked with joining and attending regular local business and industry Association events. Our sales staff also has this requirement to choose and attend an appropriate networking event at least once a month. This tactic of mixing both forms of networking has been extremely successful for us." —**Rod Andrewson, Manager of Engineering and Project Management Services, CCS Presentation Systems***

"We have a fairly sophisticated sales organization and we spend a lot of time on LinkedIn. It's about developing pros-

pects but also taking a look at their network. We also use it to keep open dialog. Same with Twitter. It's about having an open dialog, and knowing that [social media] is a good, bad and ugly sort of thing. If you're not living up to what your'e promising, your clients are going to let people know about it." —**Theresa Hahn, director of marketing and business development, Verrex Corporation**

Chapter 6:
Don't Sell Me. Show Me!

Remember the days when little work was done prior to getting the contract?

Maximum effort went into convincing the client to use your company for the work that needed to be done. Once you were chosen, the real work began.

That has pretty much gone out the window. Hasn't it?

In today's sale, the model has been completely flipped on its head.

In Todd Hewlin's recent book, "Consumption Economics: The New Rules of Tech," he simplifies this by showing two models. The first being the old sales model and the second being what he calls the "new consumption sales model."

The old model, the one many of us are more familiar with, looks like this:

- Sell it to me
- Install it for me
- Fix it for me
- Optimize it for me

Basically, sell it and own any issues for the life of the product or service. Otherwise once you put it in, you are hands-off until you are called upon.

In the new model, driven by the proliferation of Software as a

Service and Cloud, the sale looks more like this:

- Let me try it
- Manage it for me
- Drive my full adoption
- Guarantee my business outcome

With this new philosophy has come a new vernacular, a sales methodology referred to in the tech industry as "land and expand selling." The idea is that selling is no longer do customers make the majority of their decision based on a scope of work and proposal; now they seek out more empirical data to justify their purchasing decisions.

For instance, a client may be interested in deploying a new organization-wide collaboration solution. The old way would mean specification sheets, pricing, perhaps a manufacturer demo and a purchase decision.

Today's enterprise is going to be seeking something different. In the case of that same organization they be trying to give 5,000 employees access to a new cloud based collaboration tool.

The organization doesn't only want every user to have access, but they want to make sure that the solution is right and this shouldn't be based on what one or two key decision makers think. It should draw on a significant sampling of the users in the organization.

This paradigm shift means a whole new sale and sales cycle for the provider. No longer can you just win the key stakeholder and guarantee the PO.

What the organization is looking for is **User Success** and **Quantifiable Data** to back it up.

Breaking Down User Success and Quantifiable Data

Based on the new consumption model, the partner is going to provide the prospect an opportunity to "test drive" the new solution.

This will likely come after the partner has helped them through traditional needs analysis to determine one or maybe a few viable options.

At this point, the enterprise will be seeking a small, yet significant number of user accounts to test the solution. These accounts will be given to user types across a plethora of organizational roles so usability can be better determined.

At this point the vendor is going to be responsible to teach the test users how the solution works. Considering these are the product testers the goal will be to provide more than just the 50,000-foot view, but to show them how to become power users.

IT is up to the vendor partner to drive a level of user success where the organization says, "Yes, we believe this solution is viable for our business."

This isn't the end though; this is just a checkpoint for winning the deal. Remember, we have entered the "show me" economy and it takes more than a few happy users to win the enterprise.

This is where quantifiable data comes into play.

If you are anything like me, you went into sales and marketing because you were slightly overwhelmed by advanced mathematics and science.

All kidding aside, sales and marketing has become more and more science with each passing day. Have you heard about big data?

While a discussion for another time, the gist of big data is that just about everything we do can be analyzed and stored for data. **Our addiction to technology is feeding this trend and it is**

driving organizations toward more quantifiable results when it comes to their purchasing decisions.

Let's go back to the cloud-based collaboration sale we were talking about above. The 5,000-seat organization has just run a pilot for 25 users across the organization. They use the solution for video, audio and web collaboration and the users find the tool easy to use, productive and flexible.

Those are qualitative data points, but what quantitative data can we attach?

This is where the data points become imperative to the sale.

- How many meetings were held?
- What was the average length of the meetings?
- Was video turned on?
- How much data was shared?
- Were there any quality issues with the solution (latency, etc.)?

Sifting through this whirlwind of data, can you find relevancy that can help the client feel more confident in their purchase decision?

To some extent this is where traditional selling comes into play. Early on you should have been listening for queues about the challenges they were trying to overcome and how the solution you are selling can help them to accomplish this.

If you remember in the early video conferencing days, people were trying to reduce travel overhead and costs by using video. While this was good in theory, many companies bought very expensive video conferencing solutions and people didn't use them the way they thought they would. Travel costs weren't significantly reduced and companies felt burned because the investment didn't pan out.

With the data available today the use and savings could be easily calculated during the trial period and viability could have been better determined to set both better expectations and drive more desired outcomes.

Outcomes Are Key to Client Retention

Test users. Big data. Analytics. It all begins to sound like a lot of mumbo jumbo.

What can we take away and apply to our business that allows better outcomes for us? That's a fair question. If you are asking that question, your head is in the right place. In the end it is about business outcomes.

How are you going to guarantee the customer a business result if they invest in your widget or service or idea? Can you do more than tell them what they can expect, but at some point down the line show them that you delivered what you promised?

For today's solution provider, the sale isn't about the item; it is about solving a problem. We sell things to solve business problems, not thing problems. The focus must stay there if we want to successfully transition to the "show me" economy.

Our clients are seeking partners in the true sense of what partnership means. This means we are in the trenches together from the time the idea surfaces until the time it is deployed. Then we stay with them to make sure we stay on course and we work together to guide changes.

Outcomes are the currency of tomorrow's successful business. The process has changed slightly, but in the end it is always the results that decide whether or not you make the grade.

STRATEGY SHIFT: ELIMINATE BARRIERS OF ENTRY

Let's have a quick review of some hot and not items in the world of technology.

Hot: Cloud
Not: On Premise Software and Hardware Solutions

Hot: Software as a Service (SaaS)
Not: Perpetual License Based Software

Hot: Bring Your Own Device (BYOD)
Not: Appliances and Use Specific Devices

Besides the obvious fact that they are all technology related terms, what do cloud, SaaS and BYOD have in common that is driving all three of them to be "Hot"?

Before I answer, how much more likely are you to buy something when you are able to try it first?

Think about this in work and in life. Have you been to Costco over the past few years?

You walk down the aisle and it is a meal on wheels; carts everywhere with "Free" samples of Skinny Pop popcorn, chocolate covered blueberries, pork dumplings and VitaMix juice blends. My wife and I sometimes laugh about going there on the weekend for lunch because by the time we finish our shopping we are usually stuffed.

Notice the quotes I place around "free" sample.

Nothing is free. By the time you get out of Costco it is rarely under $200 (in my experience). And if you are anything like me, you wind up buying at least one thing that was on "free" sample each time you go.

The free trial once again worked and led to another conversion.

Let's go back to those technology driven items I talked about at the beginning of the story. Cloud, SaaS and BYOD — have you figured out what they have in common?

How about that each of them is a platform that allows the upmost simplicity for resellers to gain users?

How many free, freemium or free trial services are you using today?

Do you use Google Apps, Dropbox, Pandora, Base CRM, Amazon Prime, Netflix or Constant Contact? While all of these cloud-based services offer a free edition, every single one of them offers a premium (subscription service).

They also all drive revenue off of you using their free services so either you are paying to remove ads or you essentially are the product (by which ads are pushed to you).

The beauty of the model that all of these companies have is that they make it extraordinarily easy for you to try their products. In the past year I have used or I am currently using every one of those above applications and have upgraded to paid editions of three of the services. In every case where I upgraded to a paid version I started out using a free trial.

Bottom line is in the world of selling, whether it is the food you buy or the technology you consume, smart businesses are finding ways to let people try their product before they make you buy.

Can This Be Applied To Every Business?
Even if you aren't in the business of selling cloud applications or groceries, is there still a place for your business to benefit by reducing barrier to entry?

In a world where people want to try before they buy, it

should definitely be a consideration. Here are some questions to ask to determine opportunities to lower the barrier to entry.

1. What are the barriers to entry for the products and services we sell?
2. Are there opportunities for current and potential customers to become more familiar with or experience our products and services first hand prior to purchase?
3. Do we create unnecessary constraints to make it harder than necessary for a customer to try our products and services?
4. How could we set up no cost or low cost trials of our products/services?

While there are exceptions to every rule, businesses have long invested in ways to allow their customers more direct access to their offerings prior to obtaining a purchase.

Meaning even businesses that may not have a product they can completely give away have figured out ways to move their clients closer to a deliverable prior to asking for the sale.

Consider the following examples not in the Cloud/SaaS/BYOD world.

- Car dealers have offered test drives, sometimes even allow buyers to keep a car for a day or two during the buying process and CarMax revolutionized the three-day, no fault return allowing people a no question out if they opt not to buy.
- Homebuilders build model homes of the houses they are trying to sell to allow a potential buyer to imagine themselves living in the home.
- Companies like Cisco, Apple and HP build elaborate expe-

rience centers where potential buyers can visit and become immersed with technology prior to purchase.

• Numerous companies offer 30-day money back guarantees on their products and services.

Begging the question, what does your business do to make it easier for customers to engage?

Smart Businesses Find a Way

No matter what business you are in, there is a way to lower the barrier to entry and drive more customers to try what you have to sell.

The question you have to ask yourself is how much do you believe in what you sell?

If your offering meets a need and your customer experience leaves little to be desired, how risky is it to lower your customer's barrier to entry?

Given that 68 percent of defection has to do with customer service and less than 15 percent defect because of product dissatisfaction, maybe getting more customers to experience what you have to offer is the key. Just so long as your customer experience makes the grade.

SOURCES:

Talent Technologies
http://www.talent-technologies.com/new/2012/07/customer-experience-infographic

---

CAN (OR CAN'T) A SHOW-ME MODEL WORK?
By Chris Miller

A good friend once said, "While we are all in the same industry we are all in a different business." It's not a "one-size-fits-all" model and no one concept or idea will work universally to address our challenges.

As much as we need to consider the "show me" model, it's impractical to literally build a complete mockup of a client's system application. We are integrators, not manufactures of complete solutions.

However, what we *can* do is help the client understand how many critical decisions need to be made to deliver a functioning system and maintain that system at optimum performance levels for the next 24 to 36 months. This will validate our expertise and help integrator understand their clients' needs.

I am amazed how few good pictures of systems that integrators take after systems are done. In addition to having good system photos the integrator needs to get good quotes from the client — specific responses to understand the needs of the client, the deliverables, and the follow-up. That's what clients really want — assurance that you have done this before, that clients are satisfied with your deliverables and that the money invested will provide the required ROI needed.

Often the sales person doesn't ask the right questions and the client doesn't provide the right answers during the design and sales phase. The best sales and design teams will work with the client to identify the ROI required before they submit proposals. In defense of the integrator, the client has to be forthcoming of important information about the required ROI (if they actually know) and how they will measure ROI when the system is delivered. With time and talent at a premium, expertise has its cost and expectations of "show me" has to be managed.

We also need to make sure that our current clients want to be part of our evangelism team. Does the client really want a test-drive of the hardware and software or do they want a test drive of the integrator and service provider? The solutions and options are very different. It's important to help the client figure that out.

Collecting this information is one thing. Communicating it is another.

In this "don't sell me, show me" world, social media and the Internet provide opportunities for companies to share unique case studies that the client can view during the research phase of a project. It will help them recognize you and your company as understanding what it takes, the complexity of change and integration, and help to quantify what it will cost to own and maintain the system in the future.

Social media got off to a bad start with most integrators. It was immediately perceived as a "gossip" tool that would create more problems than it was worth and a time-waster at best. Today, most integrators are behind the curve and are challenged to develop consistent and relevant content to keep the social media wheels turning for their company.

Unfortunately, in some cases, integrators and service providers would rather do nothing than to do it without a long-term commitment to the program. As I mentioned earlier, the difference today is that social media is not so much a marketing tool as it is one of the most cost-effective sales tools an integrator can employ.

Alternative Ways to Ease Clients into Solutions

Creativity in deliverables is mandatory to address today's client expectations. A traditional sales model may no longer apply for a specific client's needs. While not a new concept, leasing or renting solution packages for a period of time that allow the client to test drive the concept may be an option.

Obsolescence assurance programs can also help the client feel more comfortable with their decisions. Depending on the specifics of the system, the low price point of many of today's solutions may make this a practical solution. With technology changing so rapidly the client may perceive this to be a great option and one that may be profitable to the integrator while providing the required ROI testing needed by the client.

ROI Before, During, After

I've said this many times after a client signed a large contract: "The good news is we got the order. The bad news is we got the order."

Integrators know how difficult it is to deliver complex systems. One way to make the process infinitely smoother is by keeping the relationship contact in the loop throughout the integration process and through the transition to service and support. The relationship manager is often perceived to be the salesperson; however, they don't always stay engaged as their primary responsibility is to drive sales.

So whoever the relationship manager is they need to work with the client to develop metrics with the client that can help the client identify ROI metrics before system design and later, to assess how well the system met them post-install.

Hopefully the ROI metrics are identifiable and the client is willing to share that information. There is nothing that speaks more to a client than another client who has achieved their ROI goals and speaks highly of the integrator that helped them achieve the objectives.

Chris Miller is executive director of Professional Systems Network International.

INTEGRATORS ON SELLING QUANTIFIABLE OUTCOMES

It's easy to understand that customers want a clear return on investment. Less easy to understand is how to articulate that, especially with technology solutions. Integrators explain how important quantifiable outcomes have become when talking to their clients about integrated solutions:

The folks making technology purchasing decisions are the organization's "mobilizers," **says Dale Bottcher, Western Regional VP of Sales for AVI-SPL.** *"What you're finding with these mobilizers or key decision makers is that they're more interested in the outcome or the impact a system is going to have on their organization. It's all about return on investment and improving the end user experience, driving productivity. It doesn't matter if it's black, white, green, it's just got to make sense for the organization."*

"ROI and TCO [total cost of ownership] are critical selling metrics for integration sales," **says Bruce Kaufmann, President & CEO of Human Circuit.** *"Getting the audience to prove these out is the difficult part. Technology in the recovering economy is still a discretionary corporate spend, and the only way to sell beyond basic and often under-featured systems counts on these metrics."*

"There are many other factors involved other than just revenue generation," **says Michael Boettcher, CEO of Advanced AV.** *"There is good and bad business out there, defined differently for each of us as integrators though.*

So the trick to finding the right mix is what makes us successful or not. So you have to figure out what you want to be and stick to your guns."

"Being able to prove our display real ROI or TCO is really one of the most powerful tools we have to fight against our low-cost, low margin competitors," **says Rod Andrewson, Manager of Engineering and Project Management Services for CCS Presentation Systems**. *"Being able to tangibly prove the value in spending more money up front to provide our end-users with a higher return on their investment in the lower total cost of ownership has put us ahead of our competitors many times. We have a phenomenal return customer rate I believe because we have been able to provide our customers with those two realities. How we do it, provide the information, I'll keep that a secret for others to figure out."*

"In the old days it was, 'Let's use ROI to justifying why they need video conferencing.' Now it's about how to support that video that they know they need and showing utilization rates – showing use of rooms and tying into scheduling systems," **says Bill Chamberlin, VP of Sales for Verrex Corporation**. *"I don't think a ton of integrator [leverage metrics]. In our case, I think it's really driven by our client base. They're more mature clients. They're utilizing it for their business. They expect it on AV as well as the rest of the technology they have."*

Chapter 7:
Customer Experience Trumps All Else

Where are we without our customers? What would our businesses look like? The answers to those questions are the same regardless of your business or industry.

Without customers, there is no business.

If your business operates on any other principles in the new economy then you are bound to crash and burn.

The good news is that businesses that focus on their customers have a much greater likelihood to see substantial returns on their investment.

To understand how important customer retention is, here are some staggering facts about retention.

- **Sales Probability:** Probability of selling to an existing customer 60 to 70 percent, while the probability of selling to a new customer is only 5 to 20 percent

- **Cost of Acquisition:** It Costs 6X more money to win a new customer than retain an existing customer

With numbers like these, it amazes me how many businesses spend so much time marketing to new customers while paying far too little attention to their current customers.

Relationship Between Retention and Referrals

Beyond just retaining customers, where do you think your No. 1 source of new business actually comes from?

Remember the study performed by the Business Network Institute, where it was found that 98 percent of businesses look to word-of-mouth marketing as their No. 1 driver of new business.

Again ... 98 percent! That is almost every business on the planet.

Do you remember how many of those businesses had a specific strategy to drive more word-of-mouth business?

Hopefully by now you can recall it was a horrific 3 percent!

So if word of mouth (referrals) is so important, why are so few businesses exploiting this?

It comes down to a relationship between retention and referrals. While most companies aren't actively seeking the referrals, they often still find their way to you when customer experience levels are high.

(Just imagine the possibilities if your business was to do both!)

If your clients are to recommend you, 92 percent of people will trust the recommendation. Meaning when your clients do recommend you more times than not the opportunity will come your way.

Bottom line here is the key to business growth is keeping your current customers happy.

How Important is Customer Experience to a Successful Business?

I can't even begin to tell you how often I hear that price is the largest driver in buying decisions.

While this may seem to be the case, the unfortunate truth

once again comes down to the numbers.

Question: When does price become the largest driving factor? Answer: When your business shows no meaningful differentiation

A study performed by Bain & Co, a global strategy consultancy, found that 80 percent of business owners believed their company was strategically differentiated. However, the same study found that only 8 percent of end clients saw their vendors as differentiated.

Do you see how this could drive price to be a greater factor than it should be?

When your clients see your services as interchangeable with others in the same business, price can instantly become a point of contention.

However, when you are seen as differentiated on providing top-notch customer service, pricing elasticity starts to work in your favor.

Experience Drives Profitability: Two-thirds of consumers would pay up to 13 percent more for a product or service from a vendor when they receive great customer service.

Focusing on differentiation around service may be one of the most important things you can do for your business.

Building a Customer Centric Organization

The numbers don't lie. It is obvious in the new economy where trust is perhaps the most valuable currency that we build customer centric organizations.

This leadership imperative starts at the top and migrates its way to the edges of the organization.

In my experience I have seen far too many leadership teams that are resentful toward customers and they go as far as to act as if the customers are a nuisance. Seriously, it happens.

I can recall one time sitting in a meeting with an Integrator CEO to remain nameless who said, "Our customers don't have a [expletive] clue about what they need. If they would only [expletive] shut up and listen to what we tell them, then maybe they wouldn't be having this problem right now."

Mind you, this meeting included several team members including the account executive, service manager and service technician. I can remember thinking to myself, how in the world can you expect your team to deliver best in class customer experience when they hear you, the "fearless leader" of the organization, insulting and trivializing your customers?

And I wish this was an isolated event. Behind closed doors in more than one company I have listened as top rank executives berate and belittle their customers to their peers, team members and even competitors. These behaviors set a dangerous precedent as they damage culture and promote a negative sentiment between employees and customers. In a customer centric business these types of comments should never happen, begging the question:

Has this ever been you?

As organizational leaders it is upon us to build a culture that is customer focused. This starts with the things we say and it ends with the things we do.

Companies that are customer-focused show it through their actions. Slogans like "We Love Our Customers" mean little if it's not clearly visible in the way our companies act.

The key here is building the organization to enable every employee from the CEO to the rank and file to deliver outstanding customer experiences.

This can be learned from watching companies that do it well, and by making sure that every waking moment your business is focused on delivering incredible customer experiences.

Numerically Breaking Down the Customer Experience

Still not convinced or looking for a little more fuel to light the fire of your organization? Take these numbers for a spin...

- 68 percent of customers leave because they feel you are indifferent toward them. (Note indifferent, not poor service)
- 2 percent increase in customer retention provides an average bottom line improvement of 10 percent
- 68 percent of customers leave because of poor customer service while only 14 percent leave due to dissatisfaction with a product
- Satisfied customers will tell 9 people about their good experience while unhappy customers will tell 22.
- 73 percent of consumers, who love a brand, love the brand for their service (not their product).

And finally, it always comes back to the good old 80/20 Rule (Pareto Principle)

- 80 percent of your future profits will come from 20 percent of your current customers

In the end, your business will fuel off of great customer experience and high retention rates. So while many businesses spend substantially more on marketing to new customers, maybe the best place to invest is in providing great customer experience to those you already have.

CAN WE LEARN CUSTOMER EXPERIENCE FROM AMAZON?

Empower your workforce to deliver extraordinary customer experience

Perhaps Amazon chief Jeff Bezos in his *60 Minutes* interview said it best: "Even though our pricing elasticity studies show us time and time again that we should raise prices we don't."

I mean, what is a better source of client focused inspiration than a quote from the $25 billion man himself?

In serious though, it wasn't his quote that was so profound, but rather his reasoning. Why won't he raise prices even when the economics show that they can, and that it wouldn't have a great impact on their sales?

How about this ... TRUST?

Bezo's No. 1 concern about raising prices was that the long term impact would be too great because client trust would be damaged beyond repair.

Where Does Customer Experience Stack Up In Your Organization?

If I was to ask you about client or customer experience in your organization, what would you tell me? In your memos, meetings and daily operations, how much is it talked about?

More importantly, in your daily actions, how much is your attention to creating great customer experiences showing through in the deliverable?

Companies love to analyze the data and talk about processes

that may drive better performance. One thing I hear far too little about is <u>how important the customer experience</u> is to the overall strategy.

However, in a world where seemingly everyone is just one or two degrees apart, I am astonished to find out that businesses don't make customer experience their highest priority.

According to one Forrester study, <u>only 46 percent of compa-nies even have a companywide program for customer experi-ence</u>.

So while that same study shows that 86 percent of companies call customer experience a strategic priority, the proof is in the pudding that less than half of them have an active plan in place to make sure the strategy is coming to life.

Funny thing is, I bet every one of those companies has a defined process and strategy for firing non-performers or col-lecting outstanding revenue. What makes those things more important than happy customers?

Leaders Must Enable Employees to Create Great Customer Experience.

The customer is not always right, <u>but they are always the cus-tomer</u>. So treat them well and focus on keeping them for life.

In today's marketplace even the most transactional customer can impact your business for a long time. Just think about how online reviews and lost referrals can impact any business.

One thing that every leader must know is that customer cen-tric organizations must start at the top.

It is the role of the leader to make sure that the customer is the primary focus of every activity. It is from this level of focus that profit is created.

That satisfaction drives repeat business, and it also drives new business.

As leaders though, we must position our employees and team members in situations where they can make clients happy. Talk about it often and show it in the way we engage with our clients.

Set limits and understanding for what employees can do to make sure their customers are happy. Let them know that they have your support in cases where satisfaction seems difficult to find.

In the end businesses that focus on customer first will see greater results. Amazons' Bezos may be saying it on *60 Minutes* but customers around the world are showing it every day with their wallets and the purchasing decisions that they make.

What about you? How Does your Business Focus On Customer Experience and Enabling Employees To Lead In Its Delivery?

RISKS OF MEDIOCRE CUSTOMER EXPERIENCE

I can't help but chuckle, albeit to myself, when I speak to a business owner, manager or sales person who identifies others in their industry as their only or primary source of competition.

At this point I hope it is abundantly clear that I am an avid believer that our competition comes from far more places than our industry, and further how we are far too often looking in the wrong places when it comes to determining our benchmarks for success.

When it comes to customer experience, your competition is bigger. Much Bigger!

In today's marketplace your competition for customer experience is *everyone*. How about that?

Customer experience doesn't have an industry. It is ubiquitous to consumption in every aspect of our life. And unfortunately **the only thing less memorable than a bad customer experience is an average one.**

Think about that for a minute. Do you ever go out of your way to share or talk about a completely average customer experience?

Whether you are buying a television, shopping for high-speed Internet service, or looking for a new car, we compare our best service experiences across all industries to the experience we receive during this particular transaction.

Companies like Zappos (now Amazon), Toyota and Apple are setting the bar for experience. Not just in their industries, but in the lives of their customers. And across the globe companies big and small in every market and sector are following suit. These companies are working hard to create experiences that aren't just good, but memorable.

Now the consumer expects high quality products and services at competitive pricing with a customer experience that is memorable. Easy, right?

Well, of course it isn't easy to deliver best of breed across all three of those areas, but you want to know something? The relative simplicity of delivery doesn't matter, it only matters that you do it; at least if you want to stay competitive. As Nike once said, "Just Do It."

So, am I suggesting that mediocre customer experience is actually worse than a bad customer experience?

Yes and no.

In essence, a mediocre experience trumps a bad one every time.

At least when you have a totally mediocre customer experience you never say anything about it. You will provide feedback like, "It was okay" or "Fine."

A bad experience, meanwhile, will draw a lot more out of you including details as to why the experience was bad, recommendations as to what could have been done better and, of course, the metaphoric danger sign urging others not to consume the company's goods/services.

But ironically from a branding perspective you are going to spend far more time talking about the bad experience burning the name into the mind of others. And in a highly social world where the motto "All press is good press" still has a grain of truth, your average experience gets exactly zero press.

The moral here isn't to shoot for bad because it will yield you more than average. But rather shoot for great because, unless you make memories, you will quickly be forgotten.

5 TIPS FOR CREATING UNPARALLELED CUSTOMER EXPERIENCES

Recap: An average customer experience may be the worst kind?

Yep, not a bad one, because for that you will be memorable, just not the way you hope.

However, I have long thought danger lies in mediocrity because no one remembers mediocre. But this can be overcome, and it starts by getting back to basics and realizing the sale doesn't end when you get the deal.

The point in which you win the deal is when it just begins. If you want to be remembered for being better than the rest, start by delivering better customer experiences.

Here are five ways you can create a better customer experience.

1. Listen First: We all want our customers to know we are the authority on all things technology. Our companies have all the certifications and all of the experiences with others customers just like the one you are in front of right now. However, we live in a world of mass customization, and whether we are talking about your Whopper or your car, you want it your way. Well, so do your customers. If you don't listen to them, you can only deliver it your way, which won't necessarily be what they want.

2. Set Expectations Early and Often: I believe the majority of life's disappointments are founded in improper expectations. Same goes for the integration business. With regards to technology, things don't always work exactly the way you plan and systems can be flaky for dozens of different reasons. We know this, and I think deep down most of our customers know things will never be smooth sailing. Yet we plow through the sales process promising rainbows and puppy tales. Then we try and tell customers when we run into the same set of problems, "This the first time." Kind of like what you told your parents the first time they caught you doing ... Anyhow set better expectations and you will probably deliver better results.

3. Be Thorough: Time is money, so we often try to move too quickly through the diligence stage. Quick site survey, nothing out of the ordinary and then, BAM, you get caught off guard to find the ceiling is 30 feet above the grid or you have to run plenum cable. These examples are just a couple of many that can throw a project off course. If you have ever heard the phrase, "Pay now or pay later," this is exactly what was meant. Any time you cut corners in the early phase, it usually ends up costing you your dividends on the back end. Being thorough shows the customer not only that you deliver what you say, but that you care enough to invest in the long term relationship.

4. Ask Questions: Don't wait until the end of the project to find out what the customer is thinking or how they are doing. If the customer doesn't approach you on regular interaction throughout the project, take the lead and make the request yourself. If throughout the project and the relationship you take the time to make sure that the customer is satisfied and in the know, you will be far more likely to be creating memorable customer experiences.

5. Relentless Commitment to Satisfaction: Repeat after me, "Not all projects will go perfectly." Okay, now that you have acknowledged the complexity of our business, take the next step and remember you can set yourself apart by embracing those complexities. If you have ever heard the expression, "Relationships are built in the foxhole," then you will know what I mean. But the relentless commitment is how you face problems and challenges in your customer relationship and turn them into customer experience gold.

As the service economy continues to be more and more impacted by the human interactions rather than the products themselves, businesses that set apart their customer experience delivery will win the sprint, the race and the marathon. Focusing on these simple tips is a way to make every interaction between your company and your customers just a little bit better than those with your competition.

Remember, Business People Are People
What does every business transaction have in common?

There is a buyer and seller. While the buyer and seller may be an entity, at the root of the transaction are people?

Simply put, every transaction in the world that takes place involves people.

Behind this very idea lies a substantial shift that every business, especially B2Bs, need to think about as a part of their customer experience strategy.

When we are asked to draw on examples of great customer experience, where do most of our memorable experiences come from? While I can't speak for everyone, most of my best customer experiences come from B2C (business to consumer) experiences. Maybe this has to do with the fact that customer experience is looked at more closely when we are spending our own money, or maybe it is because as individuals we engage in many service-focused activities like dining out, travel and entertainment.

Visualize the last time you received remarkable customer experience. Not just a *good* experience or a slightly better than mediocre one, but the kind of experience that is so good that you feel obliged to tell anyone that will listen.

What was it that set this particular experience apart for you?

Most likely it was an interaction between yourself and another person, right?

Have you had a truly memorable customer experience where you didn't have to interact with a person even one time? I have no doubt that such an experience is possible, even the best of those probably fall into that "slightly better than mediocre" category.

Take for instance shopping online. If you go online, buy the good and it arrives when it is supposed to, you're happy. But really, that's what you expected, right?

The Person Makes The Customer Experience Great

After much indecisiveness, I finally made the decision to buy an iMac. Being that I am fairly savvy with the technology and I was already an Apple user, I went to the Apple Store online. I picked out the machine I wanted, the accessories I wanted and I submitted the order which would be ready for pick up in three days.

Great! As long as three days from now I can go pick up my machine I am going to be really happy, although waiting three days for my self-appointed gift was a bit much.

About 24 hours later my phone rings and it was the Apple Store letting me know that my computer was ready for pick up.

Wow! This is great — only one day when I was expecting to wait three. I jumped in my car and off I went to Apple to pick up my new machine.

When I got there my computer was all ready and the "Genius" that set me up handed me his card and told me to call if I have any issues with the setup. I laughed, thinking...

1. It is an Apple, so there will be no problems.

2. This guy isn't going to help me because I didn't pay for the "Custom Setup."

3. There are a thousand people (seemingly) in this store. He won't even remember me.

Sure enough, the store employee caught on to my snark and he grabbed the card and jotted down his Cell Phone and said, "Seriously, if you need my help just call."

The setup went perfectly so unfortunately I had no need to call. However, when I finished the setup I decided to give him a call just to thank him for the offer. He picked the phone up (as he said he would). He in fact did remember me and immediately asked how he could help. I told him I didn't need help, but did want to thank him for going the extra mile.

So even though the shopping online was simple and intuitive and the install went flawless, what do you think it was that made the customer experience great?

It was the store employee that went just a little bit further to help and it made all the difference in the world.

In your business, are the folks who deal with your customers creating this sort of lasting impression?

B2B's have to recognize that it is experiences just like in the Apple Store example that are setting the bar for customer experience in every business. If the person behind the counter at the Apple Store can do just a little more to make my experience great, then B2B's large and small can take notice and put better customer experience as a top priority item.

If your business has been avoiding putting more structured focus on your customer experience strategy, you are not alone. Only about 20 percent of businesses have a well-defined customer experience strategy. However, the vast majority of the rest (73 percent) are at various stages of creating and implementing one.

No matter where you are with your customer experience, two things are for sure:

1. You need to have one.
2. Every customer experience must be considered as a benchmark.

Remember, every transaction in the world ultimately takes place between two humans. Keep that in mind when deciding how you want to create great customer experiences for those that drive your business.

SOURCES:

BNI Mid America
http://www.bnimidamerica.com/about.php

Source via Pinterest
http://www.pinterest.com/pin/188729040607902555

Source via Pinterest
http://www.pinterest.com/pin/188729040607237851

Source via Pinterest
http://www.pinterest.com/pin/188729040607008999

Keepify
http://keepify.com/retention/2013/11/05/14-customer-experience-facts-marketers-cant-ignore

E-Consultancy
http://econsultancy.com/blog/63586-just-20-of-companies-have-a-well-developed-customer-experience-strategy

---

RETENTION THROUGH TRAINING, COMMUNICATION AND INNOVATION
By Chris Miller

An absolute necessity of business today is the retention and growth from an existing customer base. This is much easier said than done in many cases and competition is everywhere — and they want your customers as badly as you want to keep them.

The bar is constantly rising on both the expectations and a true definition of that positive customer experience.

Too often we think we are providing an excellent experience but have become complacent with the existing clients we have and, in my experience, it's because we move resources away from them as we work on other projects or open up new markets. This can't happen in today's world of higher expectation and demand for timely service.

One area of opportunity for systems integrators to build up that loyalty factor is by improving your training program. Overall we do a pretty miserable job of end user training and building in a professional training model into the technology implementation program.

Why? Because we have technicians and installers doing the training and using industry buzz words that do more to undermine the learning than provide it. Bad training leads to ineffective use of the systems which leads to clients questioning both the integrator and the value of what they purchased.

The real magic happens in solidifying a client-integrator relationship when the technology is used effectively and without interruption or awkward stumbling in system usage. That operational efficiency in using the technology creates a bond with the integrator who behind the scenes has empowered the system operators to utilize all the capabilities of a system in an effective and professional manner. Your clients will develop a fierce sense of loyalty to your company when they can operate the system like a real pro and call you as needed to ask any questions on how to use the system better.

Every integrator believes they offer the best service. How do you really know that? Are there metrics and research that backs that up? Do your existing clients truly believe that your level of service warrants them not to ever shop around?

Remember even your existing clients look at your web site. Most end users won't believe it when your web site says you provide the best customer service without testimonials, statistics or some evidence that supports the claim. The reason why, is that every other website they visit says the same thing.

It's also important to note that as we move into a more IT-centric space our level of service and support is being measured against companies who deal in a mission critical environment on a 24/7 basis. The expectations will be similar and our response will need to be in accordance with that.

Innovation is the other key factor in developing customer loyalty and a constant positive experience. A sales person calling on an existing client just to see how things are going is wasting a huge opportunity to enhance the experience. I recommend a rule be put in place that if your sales person has nothing creative or innovative to offer the client in a way to help solve a business problem or save time or money, they don't bother wasting their time. Time is money and if your sales team is wasting that the experience becomes negative. Bring new and creative ideas on every visit.

I totally support the idea that creating an excellent customer experience for our existing clients is an important sales tool. I would expand that further to make it become the basis or foundation on which the company can develop a managed service and recurring revenue model. It brings forth many ways to expand the business you do with that client and opportunity to offer them more technology that what was sold in that first system.

Have your sales team become active in spotting new opportunity within that same facility, or in their other facilities, that could generate a new revenue stream, but be very cautious not to get beyond your area of expertise. I've seen that back fire many times.

Chris Miller is executive director of Professional Systems Network International.

INTEGRATORS: CUSTOMER RETENTION IS CRITICAL TO SUCCESS ... DISCUSS

"I absolutely agree. We have been preaching, and will continue to do so, to our account reps that we do not sell technology at Logic Integration, we sell an experience. And that experience has to be excellent. Of course, technology is a central part of the experience, but in the end when we leave a job, the client will most remember what it was like to work with our team. They will not remember to technical detail of what lens was chosen for a projector, or did we run a Cat 5 or HDMI directly. They will remember how they were treated, how we quickly responded to their needs, how we clearly communicated to them, and the quality of work that we provided at every stage of the project." —Bill Craig, Business Development Manager, Logic Integration

"You have to react to business with your clients. It's a way to get in there and show them how your meeting or exceeding the service agreement you have in place. You can also point out challenges, but the other thing is you get in there and you just talk about the organization and new technologies and whether they apply or not. You're adding credibly. The Internet and everything online has stripped the value out of what solution providers provide. The one thing that hasn't changed is that keeping the customer is critical. But how you go about it is completely different." —Dale Bottcher, Western Region VP of Sales, AVI-SPL

"We absolutely agree. The costs associated with recruiting new clients are ridiculously high both in time and actual cost. The after sale support is every bit as critical as the actual successful delivery of the initial system or systems. The hiatus between an original purchase and the next one can be long so maintaining the client relationship relies not just on continued communication but the level of continued service to make sure what we have sold continues to serve the client and keep their TCO low."
—Bruce Kaufmann, President & CEO, Human Circuit

"Agreed, and leveraging that story across your organization is core to success today. However, it is getting somewhat less difficult to engage new opportunities (see social media), and as our current environment continues to change, there are more reasons than ever to make the effort to find these new potential partnerships."
— Michael Boettcher, CEO, Advanced AV

"I completely agree that providing a customer outstanding customer experience creates a 'Holy Grail' situation for commercial integrators. We have an extremely high percentage of customer returns for repeat business. We currently have customers that we have been working for over 12 years. Some of our repeat customers have honored us with the opportunity to upgrade rooms that we installed for them as many as three times.

"Of course, we've also done much other work for the same customers and other venues. That doesn't happen if the customer isn't completely happy, extremely satisfied with the work that was done and the way it was done. Many of our customers are literally putting their careers in our

hands when we produce extremely complicated and mission-critical presentation systems for their organizations.

"One of the tools CCS and specifically John Godbout, our CEO, has put into place to foster the absolute best experience a customer can receive is the 'CCS experience' program for all of our employees. It is facilitated to us in the form of the game, last year a deck of cards this year a bingo card.

*"We should be tasked with providing to our internal and external customers both predetermined customer experiences and custom customer experiences throughout each month." —**Rod Andrewson, Manager of Engineering and Project Management Services, CCS Presentation Systems***

Chapter 8:
Rethinking (and Recapping) Your Market Approach

When you build your business, build your brand, how much do you think about community? Here's why you should:

About 55 percent of consumers are willing to recommend companies that deliver great experiences and 85 percent are willing to pay a premium for those services. Who are those "people" making those recommendations?

It is your community, right?

If I asked most CMOs and marketing leaders how they define their brand's community, I'm certain that I would get a different answer from each. Community being a more subjective topic will tend to yield widely varying answers.

This subjectivity is further driven by the wide variance in how different brands are seen, heard and felt by their community. More or less, how connected are they to the brand?

Think about Apple, for instance. Apple is an oft-used reference due to their powerful brand recognition, but have you considered how influential Apple's community been on the success of the brand?

Think of the last "Apple fan" or "fan boy" that you have talked to about Apple or Apple competitive products. What was that conversation like?

Chances are the conversation went wonderfully so long as

you touted how wonderful Apple products are. However, if you dare to question the products, ideas or innovation of Apple to an "Apple fan," be warned, for you have just crossed into enemy territory.

What is this insanely powerful connection that Apple has with its community? By in large Apple isn't a highly social company, so it isn't doing it in the more "Nouveau" style where it builds its army through Facebook and Twitter, etc. Apple has merely brought together a worldwide community by creating a feeling of belonging that its users get when they utilize it products.

The slogan, "Think Differently," defines a cult-like following because people who want to be seen as creative broad thinkers can often be found attached to their Macbook inside a Starbucks, almost as if the presence of an Apple defines who they are.

For Apple, this works. Through an idea of being cool, different and innovative it has built one of the tightest brand communities on and off the web.

Of course, Apple is an established "Gagillion" dollar company. How do smaller brands, newer brands tap into the power of community?

Think about the neighborhood you grew up. What was it like? Was it urban or rural? Were there many houses or just a few? Did you know your neighbors or were they merely passing strangers?

Regardless of the shape, size and geography, most neighborhoods have some sense of community. However, they aren't all the same. Where I grew up there was a "community center" which was a place where folks from the neighborhood would congregate and discuss the issues affecting the area.

The closer the community, the more they're likely to work together to get things done, things like adding a stop sign in a critical area where kids play or passing a referendum to build a new school.

When you boil it down to its most simplistic form, a community is made up of those that are stakeholders in your brand. I use the word "stakeholder" rather than "customer" because many people beyond just those that purchase your products and services can become part of a brands community. There are the obvious extensions such as employees and friends. Then there are the less obvious community builders such as those that are interested in learning more about your products and services.

When I was 14 years old (1995) my favorite car was the new Pontiac Grand Prix. They had just changed it to the wide track and as a 14 year old I thought it was one bad machine.

However at 14 I wasn't legally or financially able to buy a car. When I was 18 and I had scraped together all the loose change from under the sofa cushions and I was ready to buy a car. Guess what I bought — the Grand Prix, of course!

I had emotionally tied myself to the brand, the car, the community and when I was ready to consume it wasn't even a question who would earn my business. This type of brand loyalty can be seen to a greater or lesser extreme with everything from the food we eat to the jeans we wear and beyond.

When people become a part of something, their purchasing sentiment changes and so does the way they evangelize for your product.

If you think about the example of the neighborhood, you will usually think that a good community is small, tight knit and somewhat directionally aligned.

In the new world, the connected world where we have communities on our blog, our Facebook page, our Twitter account and on what seems like a million other places, the idea of community can become pretty daunting.

This is because the "Internet of Things" is not as big as it seems, *it is bigger*. This "massiveness" is really hard for most marketers to break down into something meaningful, often leading to brands making a few mistakes:

1. **They aim too large:** This is where they go for mere numbers (page visits, likes, followers, etc.)

2. **They don't engage:** Communicating with a digital community can seem like a daunting task.

3. **They Miss Out:** Online communities are a powerful way to build influential brand advocates, but sometimes inaction takes over when brands don't know where to start.

While these mistakes are commonly made, they can be avoided by following a few common sense tactics:

1. **Aim for Relevance:** Rather than shooting for a large community, start by aiming for those that are most likely to buy your product/service now or in the near future. Also, when it comes to online networks, especially social, find out where your target audience is and go there first!

2. **Engage More Than You Promote:** Share your stories, ideas and information, but make sure you allow the community to become part of the conversation. Ask more questions, build more testimonials and case studies. Invite participation.

3. **Start:** Even if your "start" is small, don't miss the opportunity to build a community by putting your head in the sand.

Remember that building a community can take time.

Apple does have an amazing community of insanely loyal brand advocates. It also nearly crashed and burned on multiple occasions and was saved by the innovation of how music was consumed on a tiny little MP3 player.

For most businesses not named Apple, community takes time and real work to build. This goes from the core of building products and services that your customers love to build places for them to congregate and talk about your products.

On the flip side, building communities requires brands to also acknowledge their shortcomings and respond transparently when things go poorly. Think about the kind of community rebuilding brands like Target and Snap Chat and others will have to undertake in the years following their security breaches. Neither of these incidents was purposeful by the brand, but they cost them trust and their community response will be monumental in recreating trust that may have been lost.

The beauty of community, however, is that when you build it, nurture it and engage with it, they will help your brand in good times and in bad. While never perfect — like your family, your neighborhood or your city — the community that is your brand is one of the most powerful tools in the connected world.

GOING FROM "COMMUNITY" TO "MARKET"

In the beginning of the book I asked you to imagine buying a car in the digital economy.

In your most comfortable pajamas it was just you, your iPad and an endless tunnel to the information world. In no time at all you were armed and ready to make an informed decision with the support of data, and the confidence of your trusted network.

But this really isn't anything new. The auto industry was one of the first industries that were truly revolutionized by the information age.

The example, however, is as relevant as ever. Let's take that automobile and swap it out for something else; you pick, it doesn't matter.

- Enterprise Software
- Office Furniture
- Industrial Cleaning Supplies

It can be any of these things because it isn't about what people are buying; it is how they are buying.

It Starts With Information

First and foremost customers are becoming more informed than ever before. Remember the study from Forrester that showed 70 percent (or more) of the buying cycle was complete prior to a buyer engaging a supplier?

That statistic needs to be burned into your brain because it alone is a reason to change the way you go to market.

You have to ask yourself this question: If we are not supplying the information, who is?

The role of today's B2B is to educate their customer. That is modern relationship selling. Businesses that are the source of knowledge for their clients are taking the role of trusted advisor, which is directly impacting the point at which they enter the sale.

Leading to the next question ... What are you doing to be the source of information?

In order to grab a competitive advantage, your business

needs to be driving the information to the customer.

This can be done via numerous content marketing strategies that include everything from face to face interaction to engagement on social media channels.

The key here is not to ignore the various paths to your customer and never to assume how they consume information solely based on how you consume information.

Although each industry is unique, remember you are the expert in your business. Most clients, although more informed than ever before, are dealing with a certain amount of information overload. The best business partners realize this and they help their prospects and clients to disseminate what is important from the rest in order to lead them to the best solution possible.

When you serve as the trusted advisor, and not just the fulfillment channel, you are positioning your organization to gain a sustainable advantage over the competition.

Then You Must Become More Responsive

The quickest way to undo the hard work of being the valued provider of information is to win the customer only to pay less than stellar attention to the client's needs. While many B2Bs today are still delivering service via traditional methods like inbound calls and emails, the landscape for customer service is seeing great change.

Last week when an issue arose with my cable I tweeted to Comcast and in less than 5 minutes they were on my service issue. They called me and I didn't have to wait.

This is service in the digital economy.

You may be saying that my example doesn't apply to what. Maybe. But if you decide to handle your service this way, I think that you'll find that you are wrong.

With over 60 percent of customers expecting 2 hour response times to customer service request over social media you can bet that their expectations of response from your business are growing at a proportional rate.

This is because the B2C customer who calls up their cable company or complains about a bad experience in the restaurant are the same people who run businesses and lead purchasing decisions. Just like the iPhone crept its way into business so are other consumer oriented activities, service included.

In the future we will see more businesses turn to performance based service agreements that don't tether their business partners to contracts but rather to business outcomes. We are already seeing this happen today in industries such as cell phones, an industry that once was built upon long and miserable contracts that kept clients roped in. That barrier was taken out and now customers have more no-term contract options than ever before.

Whatever industry you are in, you can expect much of the same to follow. An innovator will lead suit by making their service based on performance and you can count on downward pressures forcing others to follow.

One thing is for sure, as a business it is time to figure out how to be more responsive and more available for your clients. As performance becomes an even greater benchmark for retention you can be sure that anything less than satisfaction will be seen as unacceptable. And you can be sure customers will tell their friends.

It Is Also Time to Get More Creative

Today's companies are looking for business partners that don't stop once they inform, but they work tirelessly to help their clients innovate and drive better business outcomes. This is where information must drive inspiration ... inspired ideas, inspired support and inspired results.

With businesses in every industry focused on building whatever it is they are delivering they are counting on their partners to help fill the gaps. They need their IT providers to deliver them technology solutions that don't only drive their business, but flex and allow them to innovate.

Even if your role is selling industrial cleaning supplies you must be creative because businesses are always on the lookout for how to save time, save money and be more productive. You must always be asking yourselves, how does our business help do those things?

To be a catalyst of innovation for your customers you must focus on staying ahead of their needs, knowing the emerging trends and helping them understand how your product applies to their business. However, your role doesn't stop there. It is then that today's partner must drive verifiable adoption and then set up the customer to be able to continuously grow upon the solutions you have implemented to date.

The goal is not to sell the client once, but many times over. This is where a businesses' ability to innovate and deliver customer experience is key to putting your company in the client retention strike zone.

Whatever You Do, Stay Connected

Sadly, great products and services aren't enough. In fact only 14 percent of customers defect because a business delivers less than quality products and services.

Meaning most customers you have will stay so long as you take care of them (more on this later), but what do you do to find new customers when you are so busy trying to inform, serve and inspire those you already have? I wish I could snap my fingers, wave a wand and make it all work out, but that isn't reality.

What is reality is that 98 percent of businesses expect word-of-mouth marketing to be the No. 1 driver of new business. That's a great plan for mice and men, but not likely to be successful for most when a mere 3 percent of companies actually have a strategy to build their word of mouth.

If you want word of mouth, where will it come from?

If your answer is your network (current and past clients), you are correct and how do you gain more word of mouth? Build closer relationships with those that you serve and have served.

More or less it is time to focus your business on building its network and that building starts at the top.

The companies that will prosper most during these shifting times are the companies that focus on building the most loyal, most satisfied customers who do their selling for them.

Given that 90 percent of today's buyers trust a reference that comes from their immediate network, this isn't only a good way. It is the best way.

Other mediums don't even come close in comparison because people in general don't trust ads. It is hard to now that we are exposed to on average more than 5000 a day.

This is why it starts with networking.

Leaders need to get active in real life and online driving those relationships and building a culture that sees the value of networking. This will enable and empower the employees to become the primary brand evangelists.

Remember, your employees in many ways are like clients. They need to be nurtured and led, but once they believe in the organizations tenants they become terrific advocates to the market and they will help create more connected organizations.

However, to fully empower the employee the leader must

also give its team the proper tools to compete. This takes us back to content.

Lunch and Golf are great for relationship management, but with time being a precious commodity, our networking efforts must be moving our clients toward their knowledge goals. With so much information at their disposal, the networking activities should be focused on supplying invaluable information to help clients. This will support your efforts with all 6 of the trends because you are fostering a relationship while moving along the business.

In the end the most connected organizations will be customer activated. They will show an undeniable loyalty to customer experience (see Chapter 7). In terms of building a more connected organization this is key because no matter how well you nurture a relationship at the sales level, to truly be a purveyor of word-of-mouth, your organization needs happy customers.

It is only going to get harder to hide bad customer experiences in the future because information sharing is proliferating at such an unbelievable rate.

This All Drives a Show Me Sales Model

One thing is for sure, when it comes to customer activation a big part of the shift is going to be the expected deliverable. It is important for you to remember that the customer is expecting more in the sale process as well.

Most industries in the past had a sales cycle that looked something like this:

- Sell it to me
- Install it for me
- Fix it for me
- Optimize it for me

From this day forward it will look more like this:

- Let me try it
- Manage it for me
- Drive my full adoption
- Guarantee my business outcome

This means not only do we need to inform, serve, inspire and nurture ... Now we must stay aligned with our clients through the whole sale to help them gain organizational adoption of the products and services they sell. And perception won't be enough; data (sometimes referred to as *big data*) will be the driving force in validating that the solutions we sell indeed meet the clients' need.

Beyond just data there is another monumental shift driving the "Show Me Sale" ... The Try Me Society!

In a high-tech marketplace driven by user experiences on our second and third screens, buyers are looking for suppliers that have a way for them to test and try out solutions before buying.

Whereas, for many products in the past, a showroom or a spec sheet could serve the purpose of verification, today's business wants to take the car home and keep it for a few days, proverbially speaking.

This means businesses need to find a way to lower the barrier of entry. Essentially limit the risk of a bad decision. In the world of technology, cloud and software as a service (SaaS) this is becoming the norm, but once again those norms will drive their way into every other industry, as this will become more of an expectation. Leaving businesses to think, how can we lessen the barrier to entry without exposing ourselves to unnecessary risk?

With more of the risk falling on the providers, the key is going to be in solutions that meet the grade and service that retains.

Remember, **customers don't defect from products at near the rate they do from bad customer experience. This is precisely why companies with great customer experience can and will lower barriers to entry** both because they have to and because they want to.

The Trend of Trends: Customer Experience

While all of the trends are driving monumental shift, every single one of them can be traced back to customer experience.

Bottom line, customer retention is king and businesses that figure out how to do this better than their competition will win.

Fact of the matter is new customer acquisition costs 6x more than retention and your likelihood of expanding your sales relationship with your current clients is 60 to 70 percent, whereas selling to a new customer is only 5 to 20 percent.

This is precisely why businesses need to spend more time keeping their current clients happy. Remember, happy customers will tell about 9 others about their experience.

Not only does good customer experience drive more word-of-mouth, but it drives greater profits as well. A meager 2 percent improvement in customer retention can drive as much as a 10 percent improvement in bottom line profitability.

Moreover, the 80/20 Rule doesn't escape customer experience. In fact, 80 percent of your future profits will come from 20 percent of your *current* customers. Giving you more reason to focus on keeping them happy.

As a business the investment in customer experience will come down to driving customer-focused organizations. Much like building a connected organization, the customer-centric organization will also require the unshakable support of leadership.

Employees need to be empowered to create high levels of satisfaction in all but the most complex situations and when there is a fire in the kitchen savvy leaders need to step in and do everything in their power to keep clients.

In a world where everything other than excellent is forgettable, tomorrow's organization will fight to stay relevant with the enemy being mediocrity.

And the businesses that will win will listen to their clients, manage expectations, be thorough, ask questions that lead to solutions and show a relentless commitment to customer satisfaction.

Remember, the customer isn't always right, but they are always the customer.

What Is Your Strategy?

In the end these six trends are going to transform the way you do business. Some more subtly than others, but I'm sure if you are thinking about how you do business today you can see a little bit of all of these trends showing up more each day.

The great news is much of the transformation levels the playing field.

Bigger and older doesn't guarantee results under the New Rules of Customer Engagement.

The winners are going to be those that recognize the opportunity and focus on how they can better serve the customer.

Really all of this comes down to creating better customer experiences:

- Better Information
- Improved Response Times
- Boundless Creativity
- More Meaningful Relationships

- Well Vetted Solutions
- Customer Activated Enterprises

However, it is up to you.

Certain changes are going to impact your business more immediately while others more gradually.

In the past some companies have been averse to change, perhaps hopeful that the trends will change so they don't have to. The results of such actions haven't led anywhere good, so aversion and avoidance will never be the answer.

The very fact that you are here on this page, having read all that came before it, means that you are open to new ideas and new ways to do things differently.

At the end of the day it will always be about what is next.

Sometime very soon the words on the pages of this book will have a certain antiquated feel, as the next six trends will come to pass. However, the ambition to stay ahead of what is next will never be futile.

While we can never say with absolute certainty what is next, I look forward to the journey and I hope to see you there.

CPSIA information can be obtained at www.ICGtesting.com
Printed in the USA
LVOW04s1400061114

411804LV00002B/3/P